SADISTIC PLEASURES

Silent Crimes of Azerbaijan

by ASHKHEN ARAKELYAN

For permission requests, write to the publisher at contact@identitypublications.com. For media inquiries, write to the author at silentcrimesofazerbaijan@gmail.com.

Library of Congress Control Number: 2022900770

Ordering Information:
Quantity sales. Special discounts are available on quantity purchases by corporations, associations, and others. For details, contact the publisher at the address above.

Orders by U.S. trade bookstores and wholesalers. Please contact Identity Publications: www.identitypublications.com.

ISBN-13: 978-1-945884-55-9 (ebook)
ISBN-13: 978-1-945884-56-6 (paperback)
ISBN-13: 978-1-945884-57-3 (hardcover)

Cover designed by David Vardanyan. The cover depicts a human eye rolled up and back toward the skull. The two most common times this exaggerated expression occurs are during death and orgasm. Hence, appropriate to the title and theme of this book, it is a potentially profound symbol of both sadism and pleasure.

First published by GevorgVirats in Georgia.
Second Edition
Publishing by Identity Publications.
www.IdentityPublications.com

PRAISE FOR *SADISTIC PLEASURES*

The Forty-Four Day War over the Nagorno-Karabakh/Artsakh region in 2020 marks the latest outbreak of manifest violence in a history of the conflict that goes back more than a hundred years. Its current starting point began with the end of the USSR, with the brutally waged armed conflicts between 1992 and 1994 and the declaration of independence of Nagorno-Karabakh. With the ceasefire of November 10, 2020, the fighting ended. Unfortunately, the suffering of the people affected by that war, marked by excessive violence, did not. The physical and psychological injuries and the losses of family members and friends will forever accompany those who lived through the violence.

Sadistic Pleasures makes such experiences accessible to us. It offers devastating insights into the dynamics of violence defined by a national hatred handed down over many generations, by distrust of one's neighbor, driven by the need for revenge.

Ashkhen Arakelyan has conducted interviews with Armenians who fell captive to the Azerbaijani militias and military forces in the last Karabakh war: sometimes as soldiers but often as civilians who found themselves between or behind the lines by mere chance. Fourteen of these stories are included in this book: haunting accounts of the experience of physical and psychological torture, of fear and uncertainty in the face of impending death, of pain, loss of direction, humiliation, and degradation. Ashkhen Arakelyan has carefully edited the interviews while preserving the character of the immediacy of the accounts. With short insertions and commentaries, she succeeds in conveying the narrative situation, the peculiar atmosphere of the conversations in which the interviewees reported on their experiences of violence.

Reading this book highlights the chasms of violence to which nationalism leads and invites us to empathize with the victims. It also demonstrates the helplessness of human rights organizations in the face of perpetrators who are determined to dehumanize those at their mercy, to cause them lasting physical and psychological harm. This book prompts us to make an emphatic commitment to humanity and sincere adherence to the principles of international humanitarian law. *Sadistic Pleasures* is an indispensable source, valuable documentation from which to draw a sense of the inexplicable.

—Dr. Mihran Dabag, The Institute for Diaspora and Genocide Studies

Starting with the Nuremberg Trials in 1945, the international community agreed to punish international crimes, including war crimes, crimes against humanity, and genocide. Behind these gruesome crimes are hundreds of lives, numbers of victims, numerous pains, and a wealth of individual stories. Very often, when journalists, politicians, lawyers talk about the international crimes that were committed during conflicts, they talk about "victims" in abstract. What is forgotten, however, is that every victim of large-scale crimes is a person who has a name and who has suffered individual harm as a result of international wrongdoing. Ashkhen Arakelyan shows in her well-documented publication the individual victims behind international crimes.

Arakelyan portrays the victims who were targeted because of their identity and not because of their personality: targeted because they were Armenians. These individual stories tell the reader about hatred of the Armenian ethnicity, that the victims were victimized not because of their goodness or malice but because they belonged to a certain group of people. They tell of the physical and psychological damage the victims suffered during their captivity.

This publication is not only an important documentation of individual fates but also a source of evidence of international crimes committed before, during, and after the Forty-Four Day War in Artsakh in 2020.

—Dr. Gurgen Petrossian, LLM (Heidelberg), Senior Researcher, Head of International Criminal Law Research Group at Friedrich-Alexander Erlangen-Nuremberg University; Chairman of German-Armenian Lawyers' Association

TABLE OF CONTENTS

FOREWORD FROM THE PUBLISHER

Sadistic Pleasures was first published in late 2021 in Armenia and Georgia, almost exactly one year after the Second Nagorno-Karabakh war began. It became clear then how important it was that these stories be made accessible to the rest of the world in the interest of fair and open journalism about a sensitive and important issue that the powers that be go to great lengths to keep hidden.

I am an American of partial-Armenian descent from California who became repatriated in Armenia in 2019. Thus, it was particularly important to me that Armenians and their descendants in the Western world get a sense of the firsthand experience of what has been going on in this part of the world that they are emotionally and culturally connected to but physically insulated from.

In September 2020, I was living a peaceful life in my village home in Kalavan in the Gegharkunik province of Armenia when news of the war with Azerbaijan over Artsakh reached my neighbors. For a month and a half, we waited each day to hear developing news of the potential for escalation and whether our village, being only an hour or so from the border with Azerbaijan, would be under threat from bombing or military invasion.

The reality of life for Armenians living so close to neighbors with ambitions of territorial expansion fully hit me when my teenage neighbor stopped by my house to urge me to keep all my lights off at night in case drones operated by the army of Azerbaijan would be patrolling the area at night looking for populated areas to strike for the purposes of inducing terror and demoralization among Armenians. The fact that this request did not seem strange or terrifying to him made me wonder how my American friends back home might react to what would be an unthinkable situation to residents of a politically and militarily secure nation like the USA.

During those awful six weeks and in the year since, I have been witness to endless state-sponsored internet propaganda put out by those who control the official political narrative in Azerbaijan. Those Armenians who attempt to call attention to what is really going on have been attacked by ordinary Azerbaijani people for daring to even call into question whatever the government tells them is the truth. However, the fate of independent journalists attempting to report the truth within Azerbaijan has been far worse.

There was and continues to be an information war raging around the world about exactly what happened and who is at fault for countless crimes committed in the name of political agendas. During the war, Azerbaijan's internet access quickly became heavily censored by its own government.[1] Even now, Reporters Without Borders (RSF) ranks Azerbaijan quite low at number 167 out of 180 in their press freedom index[2] and condemns the country for its rampant jailing of journalists who dare speak out against their sanctioned version of history and their present actions. It should be no surprise then that what really goes on during times of military conflict and how POWs are treated remains hidden from public knowledge both domestically and abroad.

For any citizens of Azerbaijan or their descendants who read these accounts of the inhumane actions sanctioned by their military and political leaders, there may be great emotional resistance to accepting them at face value. I urge you to try to avoid interpreting these accounts as attacks upon your personal identity and values. It should be clear that there are individual people responsible for these crimes and that no reasonable person blames a collective for the orders and acts of men who operate above reproach. To take pride in your national identity is to

---

[1] https://tvrain.ru/news/vlasti_azerbajdzhana_ogranichili_dostup_k_internetu_posle_obstrelov_v_karabahe-516731/
[2] https://rsf.org/en/azerbaijan

demand the best from those people in power who represent your nation to the world, just as, hopefully, Armenians will continue to demand the truth and upstanding moral action from their leaders too as this situation unfolds.

Anyone who is forced to form their worldview under conditions of strict informational control and take violent actions at the behest of politicians is, ultimately, as much a victim as the innocent people hurt by these actions. National pride and cultural ideology, therefore, can be dangerous things when evaluating the truth during tense and conflicted situations. It is only by bringing uncomfortable facts to light that we can eliminate inhumanity and raise everyone to a higher standard in chaotic times. As individuals of any nation, creed, or religion are capable of great evil, it is our duty to call out perpetrators, no matter how we might identify with or against them, with the complete journalistic integrity made possible by freedom of the press and media. That is what Ashkhen Arakelyan has accomplished in this collection of suppressed real-life accounts of great evil going on in our modern world.

Freedom of expression is an essential part of how we form reasonable and accurate opinions about what is going on in the world. Those who probe into hidden issues, ask difficult questions, and dismantle barriers to honest communication further this endeavor for the global human populace. Though I am no journalist by profession, I value free inquiry and investigation as one of the highest societal goods. Indeed, that is the reason I started Identity Publications in 2016: to enable unknown authors to share their important messages. I have made it a personal mission to make Ashkhen's important efforts more widely available to the global public (and particularly to those who care back in my home country) so that these barbaric practices may be tolerated no longer, wherever they may occur.

It is my perception from living here these last three years that Armenia is a nation that has long struggled to have a proper voice upon the stage of the world. I hope you read these stories and choose to do something small but meaningful toward raising awareness outside yourself about what is happening in this ancient but important land.

Gregory V. Diehl, Identity Publications
Kalavan, Armenia

BRIEF HISTORICAL OVERVIEW

The area known as Nagorno-Karabakh (called "Artsakh" in Armenian) was inhabited by the people of the Early Transcaucasian Culture in prehistoric times. Strabo mentions the area as "Orchistene." In the sixth century BC, the area came under the rule of various Iranian empires (the Medes and Persians). By the second century BC, Artsakh (Karabakh) had become a part of the neighboring Kingdom of Armenia. From that time on, the fate of Artsakh was closely bound up with that of Armenia. It is, however, possible—albeit disputed—that its native inhabitants were originally Caucasian Albanians (entirely unrelated to the Balkan Albanians), although they mainly lived further north in Caucasian Albania.

At any rate, both Armenia and Artsakh were mostly associated with the Iranian empires in one way or another during much of antiquity, be it as a satrapy of Persia or as a vassal state. From the first century BC onwards, the area frequently changed hands when the Romans and Iranians (Parthians and Persians) fought over it, interspersed with periods of relative Armenian self-sovereignty.

An important event was the adoption of Christianity as the state religion of both Armenia and Artsakh (the first official national conversion to Christianity in world history) in the early fourth century, from that time onwards, particularly after the invention of the Armenian alphabet and the considerable geographical spread of Armenian culture in the fifth century, the inhabitants of Artsakh were gradually Armenianized. Notably, the church of Caucasian Albania was a subordinate entity within the Armenian Apostolic Church, which further illustrates the Armenian influence in the wider area. Later, the whole Caucasus, including Artsakh, was incorporated into the Arab Caliphate—but remained Christian.

Eventually, the Turkic Seljuks conquered the area in the mid-11th century. Thus, it was only a thousand years ago that Turkic people(s) started gradually to migrate into the Southern Caucasus over the following centuries. The Turks called Artsakh "Karabagh" (a mixed Turco-Persian word meaning "black garden;" the later Russian prefix "Nagorno" means "mountainous" and the spelling "Karabakh" is a Russification of "Karabagh") from the 14th century onwards. Like the rest of the Middle East, Armenia and Artsakh were dominated by the Turks and Mongols until 1501, when Persia took over again. Karabakh remained under Persian rule until Persia was obliged to cede its land north of the River Araxes—including both Armenia and Karabakh—to the Russian Empire in the treaties of Gulistan (1813) and Turkmenchay (1828).

The demographics of the South Caucasus slowly began changing during the centuries following the Turkic conquest, with Turkic Tatars spreading their language all over the area and Turkic rulers redrawing administrative borders. The region, which later became the Republic of Azerbaijan, became the most heavily Turkified part of the South Caucasus—with the notable exception of Karabakh, which always retained a significant Armenian majority, and the Caspian coast, where Iranian ethnicities remained. In the Tsarist maps of the 19th century, the (often nomadic) Turkic tribes living in the Caucasus were still called "Caucasian Tatars."

However, in the wake of the nationalist awakenings of the late 19th century, Turkic intellectuals in Baku began to propagate the idea of a common Turkic national identity for the people of the South Caucasus, and they chose the term "Azerbaijan" for their envisioned nation. This choice was politically motivated: Azerbaijan (a Persian name) had always exclusively denoted a north-western region of Iran/Persia (as it does still today), which was and is an entirely separate entity than the areas north of the river Araxes, the area of the later-to-be-established Republic of Azerbaijan. Since large swaths of north-western Iran had also become Turkic-speaking by this time, the greater vision behind the appropriation of this name was to conquer north-western Iran and form a greater Turkic nation-state and the local Turkic "Azeri" identity.

The early 20th century saw the decline of the Russian Empire, the Bolshevik Revolution, and, hot on its heels, the establishment of the Soviet Union. With the Russian authorities losing power in the South Caucasus during these upheavals, Armenians and Tatars began to clash in Karabakh. In 1918, the Azerbaijan Democratic Republic (the name chosen for political reasons) was proclaimed to exist alongside the Armenian Democratic Republic, and there were soon clashes between Armenians and Tatars (henceforth officially called "Azeris") in the border region that was Karabakh, culminating in the massacre of Shushi (or Shusha), where about 20,000 Armenians were massacred by Tatars (Azeris) in a most brutal manner.

Soon afterward, the entire Caucasus was incorporated into the Soviet Union. When, in 1921, Karabakh was assigned to the Armenian Soviet Socialist Republic (since its inhabitants were mainly Armenians), Stalin intervened one day after that decision and reassigned Karabakh to Azerbaijan—again for political reasons (divide and conquer). This awarding of the territory to Azerbaijan in the initial throes of the Soviet Union laid the foundation for the Karabakh War at the time of the USSR's dissolution in the early 1990s. Although Armenians and Azeris coexisted (relatively) peacefully during the seven decades of Soviet rule, the 20th century did see several episodes of ethnic cleansing through deportations by both sides. As regards Karabakh, the Azerbaijani Soviet Socialist Republic pursued a policy of increasing the Azeri population in Karabakh in order to change the demographic balance in its favor. The Armenians, on the other hand—being well aware of the many atrocities recently committed against them by Turkic peoples, most notably the Armenian Genocide of 1915 by the Turks (whom the Azeris consider their brothers), and conscious of often having been made a minority in their own lands—resisted the Azerbaijani SSR's policy of Turkifying Karabakh by degrees.

During the final years of the Soviet Union, ethnic conflict flared up again, and soon a series of pogroms were carried out against Armenians in Azerbaijan proper, the most significant and brutal episode being the Sumgait pogrom near Baku. Soon, the Armenian population of Azerbaijan was expelled or fled to Armenia and vice versa: all Azeris in Armenia were deported to Azerbaijan. Finally, the First Karabakh War in 1988–1994 resulted in the loss of the area by the Republic of Azerbaijan and territorial control of Karabakh by Armenia. The outcome was a "frozen conflict:" for 26 years, Karabakh was internationally recognized (de jure) as part of Azerbaijan, but (along with the immediate area around it) a de facto independent republic whose security was guaranteed by Armenia.

On September 27, 2020, Azerbaijan, heavily assisted by Turkey and by imported members of Syrian jihadist terrorist groups and unprecedentedly using advanced drones of Israeli manufacture as well as availing itself of army supplies and élite troop training from various Muslim nations, began a unilateral offensive military campaign, resisted largely not by the Armenian army but by local militias of Artsakh and volunteers from Armenia. The 44 days of fighting resulted in an agreement on November 9, 2020 between Armenia, Azerbaijan, and Russia as broker, in which Armenia agreed to cede not only those areas that had just been lost during the military campaign but also other territories of Nagorno-Karabagh proper, as well as all newly-conquered areas (including the strategically and symbolically vital hilltop city of Shushi) to Azerbaijan, with Russian peacekeepers to be stationed henceforth in Karabakh.

At the time of this publication in early 2022, the Azeris continue their military campaign (in breach of the agreement) and have intruded into the border regions of Armenia proper, their apparent (and stated) goal being the conquest of the Zangezur corridor: the very slender southern Armenian province of Syunik that represents the only non-Turkic territory in a contiguous band between Greece and China.

CHAPTER 1

The Cruelty No One Could Measure

My brother drove me to meet Narek (S.). I was a bit nervous. I'd known Narek since childhood. Although I had believed that my connection with the people of my village had weakened during the many years since I had left, when I heard the news that the Azeris had captured Narek, I lost my peace until he returned. His story was larger than life, hard to swallow.

It was rather cold at Narek's place. In the bed on the corner, there was his dad, suffering from cancer. The kids were the reason the house was still breathing. Everyone looked radically old. Everyone seemed exhausted: from sufferings, from never-ending problems, from each other. At some point, I asked to be alone with Narek.

> I farm for a living. This year we decided to breed the cattle in a different area. Before starting the day, I thought I'd call my family first. The network was bad in that area, so I had to climb up the mountains to get a signal. I could see a military base around 300 meters away from where I was standing. I thought it must be an Armenian base, as did other farmers around me. I couldn't get through to my wife, so I started back down again.

Narek was 30 years old. All his life, he was renowned for his farming—and he enjoyed it. He had a wife, two kids, and enough money to get on with life in an abandoned village.

> Before I could even take a few steps back down the hill, someone called to me. I turned around; I realized a

soldier was talking to me in Russian. I thought at first that he was an Armenian soldier, probably drunk and trying to make fun of me. I ignored him and continued walking. I'd almost reached my horse and was about to mount it when I realized four fully-armed soldiers were approaching me. They crossed the trench and came up to me. I kept standing there, still thinking they were Armenians. In my head, I was calculating what I would tell them if they asked me my reason for being up there. The closer they got, the more clearly I heard them speaking Russian. For a moment, I thought they must be Russian peacekeepers, but never did I imagine they were Azeris. The moment came when they were so close that I could see their boots and the flag on their military uniforms. I was frozen stiff. I realized they were our enemies. Never had I this feeling in my life, the feeling of going numb. I lost my ability to do anything. I just stood there, fixated on their eyes.

I hoped I'd be able to talk to them. I hoped to negotiate. For the first two minutes we spoke, I told them I would never go back there again and that I'd just been trying to get a phone signal. It was in vain. They blindfolded me, and I had to go with them. Two held my arms, one was leveling a weapon at me from behind, and off we went. I begged them; I tried to find some arrangement with them. However, we had already crossed the trench, and I had left the Armenian border behind. I had still not fully realized I was a captive. On the other side, as they talked in Azeri, the reality changed. I couldn't accept what a life-changing mistake I'd made. I was only 30, and my life was over while I was still in my prime.

Narek was lowering his voice to make sure the occupants of the next room were not upset. He didn't look into my eyes as he started sharing his story. Maybe it was shameful for him to share his story with a girl, especially when that girl had known him since childhood. However, after a while, he started getting used to my questions, and the conversation became less tense, more back-and-forth.

They opened my eyes, and I was devastated to see an enormous Azeri flag hang on the building in front of my eyes. Quick as a flash, they put a bag over my head and led me to a dark room. The interrogation started right away. They confiscated my phone, took the bag off my head, and then started beating me up. As they were likely to claim some military angle to any picture found on my phone, I knew they were going to torture me. I couldn't speak their language, nor could I speak Russian well. I could barely explain anything or communicate with them. After a while, they blindfolded me again, tied my hands, and took me on a three- or four-hour drive. I couldn't eat, although they offered me some food. I was scared they would try to kill me by lacing the food with something. I hoped it would only be a matter of hours before I was home again. I hoped the Armenians would help me get back within a couple of days.

Instead, I landed in Nakhichevan Prison. Here, the nightmares started. The cell had no bed, no windows, literally nothing. The whole building was dark green. On the second floor, there was President Aliyev on the wall, a huge portrait. His father's portrait was hanging beside it. The first cell I occupied, until November 23rd, had no windows; it was very damp and smelt of apples. There were also some sugar sacks on the floor; I thought it was an old warehouse. Only for the last 20 days was I in a proper room.

After around ten days, the Azeri officials started driving me from one place to another for interrogation.

They always blindfolded me; even when they took me to the toilet, I had to be led all the way around it three or four times to disorient me. I had around 150 contacts stored on my phone, and during interrogation, they would go through each number, asking every last detail about that person.

They used an interpreter, as I had zero ability in any other language but Armenian. The interpreter told me that his neighbor was an Armenian and had helped him learn the language. During the first war in the 1990s, he had gone to the Azeri exclave of Nakhichevan, converted to Islam, and had never returned to Armenia again. After interpreting for me, he suggested that I should stay there as well. I told him I wanted to go back to my kids. That was the day when it got through to them that I had no intentions of staying there.

As Narek was my first interviewee, everything he would tell me shocked me. I couldn't have imagined that inducing Armenians to stay in Azerbaijan and proselytizing them to change their religion was one of the scenarios that would come up again in other interviews I conducted. Perhaps preparing questions in advance was the silliest thing I could have done for this project; each of the interviewees had a unique story to share, and as soon as we struck up a conversation, the questions would flow naturally. I was floored by Narek's next detail, which was the most compelling one to me.

The next day, the Azeri officers wrote a report saying that reason I'd had to travel 100 kilometers to find good pasture for the animals was that the Mayor of Goris had taken all the fertile lands for himself and given me the most useless tract to breed my cattle on. They also made me say that the Armenian Government was brutal to me, that the police discriminated against me, and many other such accusations. And they were going to make a video of me reading out that text and spread it on the internet. I had no choice but to say it; otherwise, the torture would have become more severe.

I had only half an hour to learn the text by heart. I couldn't manage in such a short time, and I would utter three to four sentences, then forget the rest. At that, they would start beating me, torturing me, accusing me of not wanting to say my lines. But somehow, I was able to make them understand that I needed more time to learn the script. Next, they poured petrol on my feet and told me they would set fire to them if I refused to talk in the video. Then, I intentionally refused to record the text for two days because I wanted them to kill me, so the torture would end. But it dawned on me that if the video was released, my family would see I was alive and could try to help me. Thus, because of this video, the International Committee of the Red Cross (ICRC)[3] visited me after 29 days of captivity.

Narek was captured on July 8, 2020, before Azerbaijan launched its war against Armenia on September 27th. What I witnessed through Narek terrified me and will do for the rest of my life. The Azeris were extremely brutal; perhaps the severe hatred they bore against Narek (and against Armenians, generally) had been there before they won the war. Narek was and would always remain the "best" example of the extent of the Azeris' cruelty.

It was August 5th. The guards took me to a cozy cell where I had a table, a TV, and even a bed for the first

---

[3] "Red Cross" is the short form of the name of the ICRC used by the Armenian ex-POWs during the interviews.

time in a month. I waited there to meet the Red Cross. One of the visitors asked if it was my cell, and I had to say yes because as soon as they left, the Azeris would kill me if I'd told the truth. The representative opened his bag and took out some documents; I noticed two photos of my younger son. I thought maybe he had it from Facebook. I didn't dare to look up, but out of the corner of my eye, I could see two letters. I was transfixed to see that they were written in Armenian. I read my wife's name on them, and at that moment, I had my whole strength back again.

I went for the letters like a madman and opened them to read. When I read "Dear Narek." I fainted—not that I realized that at the time. After 20 minutes, when I had regained consciousness, I realized everyone was in a panic. Doctors and officials were running in different directions. The Red Cross officer had broken out in a sweat, and he was clearly distraught and terrified. I grabbed the letters and continued reading them. Receiving those letters was the only light I had during these six months of captivity. Before I read the letter, I had thought of ending my life—but I had no idea how I would accomplish that, as around five men were posted in front of my cell and would open the door every 15 minutes.

The kids returned from kindergarten. Narek's face brightened as the children entered the room. It was because of these tiny creatures that Narek, the captive, had found strength within him. A second earlier, he had been talking about suicide; now, he was hugging his children and exuding positivity.

It was snowing outside, and I had only one T-shirt and a very light pair of trousers. Whenever someone was on the way to see me from the Red Cross, they would bring warm clothes and take me to the nice cell again. I couldn't say anything to the Red Cross. They had a list full of questions about my conditions of captivity to run through in Armenian. The representative would ask if the Azeris were giving me water to drink, and I would say yes; he would write down the answer. He would then ask if anyone had tortured me and if I could show them any marks; I would say no. Then, whether I needed a doctor. I would say no, and so the list of questions went on. There was no way I could tell them the truth.

Even though I said nothing to the Red Cross, the Azeris would start beating me as soon as the visitors left. Once, the Red Cross brought two bags full of food and clothes. I told them I didn't need them. They took the bags out to the corridor and told the guard that they were for me. As soon as they left, the guard opened the bag, took out a can of Tushonka beef stew, and threw it at me. It hit my ankle and opened a gash. From that day until my release, my wound was festering and swollen.

It was August 8th. They were in the mood to try something new. The officers heated a kebab skewer and stuck it in my leg. No particular reason; nothing special had to happen to turn them violent. That evening, five or six of them gathered and came into the cell to humiliate me. There was not a single day that I could recall as the nicest. Maybe just one. On November 23rd, one of the generals entered the cell, and he realized I was very close to death. My hands were black; my whole body was covered in bruises, which were no longer blue but already black. Everyone who passed my cell would enter, draw his baton, and start on me. They would drag me back and forth, beat me until I fainted. Then they would throw me back into the cell without bringing me back around to consciousness. I would come to, cough, and feel utterly drained. Then during the night, the same scene would repeat itself.

When the general entered my cell that day, he was shocked to see my condition. For my part, I was petrified and thought this day would be my last. Then he commanded the guards to take me to the nice cell. He drew his baton, came closer to me, and put the baton down on the table. He told me to take my T-shirt off. He observed my torso as I stripped and flew into a rage at seeing it completely blackened. He picked up his baton and threw it at another officer guarding the door. He ordered them to treat all my bruises within six hours. As he left, the doctors were already bringing me a special medicine, and after three days, I was like a well man again, without any traces of brutalization.

The reason the general was being nice to me was that a Red Cross visit was imminent. As the Red Cross got to my cell, they were very insistent and told me to take off my clothes because they wanted to be sure the Azeris weren't torturing me. So I took my clothes off, and there was nothing to be seen. That general had had advance knowledge that the Red Cross would visit me, and within one day—literally one day—the doctors saw me five or six times, looked at the bruises, and made sure my body was healing.

But one of the doctors was the nastiest man in the whole jail; his son had been a soldier, and the Armenians had killed him in January. He was full of hate and vengefulness, and he took it all out on me. One of the guards was also very brutal. He told me that the Armenians had killed his mother in front of his eyes when he was 12 years old and his sister only eight. Also, the Armenians had killed his grandmother in the garden, and they both saw it happen. These were enough reasons for them to let the hatred out.

Did you believe their accounts?

> I would say yes. I had the feeling that that doctor and
> guard were filled with hate; they would enjoy watching
> me scream and wail. I would sweat from pain, they saw
> my heart was about to give out, but they would go on.
> They'd been waiting for the chance for years, and they
> finally had an Armenian, had all the freedom in the
> world to exact their revenge. They even got tired and
> sweaty from it—but as they were beating the life out of
> me, I could see the pain in their eyes.

Narek had empathy. He understood and even justified his torturers. He was full of pain, confused, and depressed, but during the
whole conversation, he repeated: "I could feel the doctor's pain."
Narek will never get over the past. As the Forty-Four Day War
ended, Narek's village found itself on the frontier with Azerbaijan. The Azeri soldiers were ensconced just a few yards from
Narek's house. The window in the living room had a bullet graze
from Azeri fire during the war. This mark on the window was
the most exciting thing for Narek's youngest son, and he was
very eager to show it to me. The children were constantly talking
about the war, the sound of the artillery, the enemy being very
close. I wonder what Narek felt when listening to his children's
conversation.

> Each time the Red Cross visited me, they asked me if
> I needed anything. But because they repeated this re-
> frain every time they visited me, I stopped holding out
> any hope. What's more, as soon as they would leave,
> the Azeris started saying a death sentence awaited me.

Could you make out the voices of any other captives?

> No. In Nakhichevan, there were no other prisoners of
> war. There were some Azeri detainees but no other

Armenian captives. I was completely alone in my cell. The days did pass by very fast, though. They tortured the hell out of me. I had to stand for 20 hours a day, and I had no opportunity to sit. Some were a bit kinder and would let me lean against the wall but never to sit. Then I would lie on the floor, and if they were nice, they would let me use my flip-flops as a pillow; otherwise, I had my arms.

There were times when I was kept awake for three days in a row. I was not allowed to close my eyes. Some of the guards did have a heart—but were powerless. There was a camera in my cell; even if they wanted to help me, they couldn't. When they were drinking tea with baklava, I would ask them to give me just a corner of a sugar cube. The guards would open the door and throw it on the floor as if I was a dog, or they would pretend to be coming to beat me up and would throw five or six fragments of sugar cubes on the floor. But they would intentionally harden the bread by drying it, so I couldn't bite it. They would put some salt or pepper in the tea and mock me as they stood and watched me drink it. They would give me their leftovers: some dry bread and some water in the afternoon. Sometimes, I would wait until they were distracted by something, and I would soak my crust in water to make it edible. In October, during the war, they stopped feeding for three days, and then they would bring me food for two days again and then stop for another three days.

Whenever the officers were bored, they would start torturing me. Then they would leave for an hour or two, and I would start mentally counting the inhabitants of my village until they re-entered the cell and started the torture again. When the Red Cross visited me, they brought me some books. One of the books was *The Little Prince*. It wasn't until December that I got the book, and I finished it in two days and then re-read it many times until the day I was let out of the cell.

I also thought that the Red Cross was well able to see how my condition was worsening by the day. They could see bruises all over my hands, but as I told them that everything was fine, they would write that answer down. Every time the Red Cross visited me, the Azeri soldiers would give me a long-sleeved shirt and another garment on top to cover my neck and torso. With the Red Cross' help, I wrote two letters and made a one-minute video for my family. I also received eight or nine letters, but I wasn't allowed to take them back to the cell with me. I had to read each one then and there and hand it back to the guards. Then, every ten days, they would give it to me again and grab it back off me a few hours later. Actually, I was glad they kept the letters because I had nowhere in the cell to keep the letters but the bare floor.

They were extremely bloodthirsty for torture. If some Azeri wandered across the border and I had the chance to torture him, I would maybe do it to him that same day, just to vent my anger. But these people had so much hatred and anger that they would come every other hour, recharged and ready to torture me some more. Someone would call and order the guards to start beating me, and they would just lay in without tiring. The commander would sit on the third or fourth floor, phone the guards, and command them to start the beatings and make sure he could hear my screams in his office. They would tie my hands, so I had no chance of shielding myself from the blows.

The electric shocks were the worst experience I had. The moment they turned the electricity on, my heart would leap out of my chest. The smoke would fill the room. They used it on my body: my hair would burn, I got heart pangs, I would lose my mind, but it wouldn't stop them. There were two electric shock devices, one with a battery and the other with iron fangs, which was not as painful. The one hooked up to the battery burned very intensely: I would feel it going right through my bones. There was never a reason for such behavior; they did it for fun. When I couldn't bear the pain anymore, I would pass out; then, they would wait a while before throwing water on my face. They would drag me over the floor and then clean the mess on the floor. Each of them was highly physically trained and weighed around 130 kilograms. I always looked at their shoes, and if they were wearing trainers, I was in luck that day. Kicks from that footwear didn't hurt as much, even if they hit my forehead. Army boots were the most painful, and I would cry for days afterward. One day, they told me they were going to pull out my nails, so I started gnawing them short with deep bites. I was terrified."

He took a deep breath, full of pain.

I was in for 161 days. I counted the hours. The month of October was the worst. They had their TV on, and I would hear how they celebrated a battlefield victory almost every day. They would come and tell me how many deaths the Armenians had incurred. As the war escalated, they started coming into the cell and torturing me severely. They turned the volume up and made me watch how they were wiping out Armenian positions, soldiers and artillery. During the first week of the war, they would take me out to the corridor and beat me. They thought they were going to lose the war, as, in that first week, the Armenian soldiers were putting up a strong defense. They were worried and became extremely brutal toward me.

Then, a week later, they started asking me if I knew where Qubadli or Jabrayil was, and when I said I did, they would reply that the town wasn't under Armenian control anymore. I thought they were making fun of me; I didn't really take them seriously. But their spirits were rising by the day. I could imagine them perhaps taking Zangilan, but never Qubadli. They even asked me if I'd ever been to Qubadli, and when I said yes, they went wild and started tossing me left and right. I was scared because I thought if they'd really managed to take Qubadli, that meant my village would be next: my family, my children. I had no news about the situation in my village. The Azeris were always telling me that they'd killed so many Armenian soldiers that day, loaded the corpses onto a KAMAZ truck, and dumped them somewhere in Azerbaijan. I couldn't believe it.

I was becoming full of rage at them. The guards told me the reason for their hatred of me was the Armenian slaughter of kids and women way back at Khojaly. They truly believed that Armenians hated them and had killed civilians at Khojaly. I didn't believe them because I'd heard that the Azeri Government had organized that massacre themselves and pinned the blame on the Armenians. But as they had an unshakeable belief that the Armenians were responsible for it, I could understand their hatred and how blinded they were by hatred and pain.

On top of that, we had occupied some of their territories for around 30 years. These people had dark emotions and had been under their government's propaganda for 30 years: I had to pay for their pain. I wanted them to kill me; yes, I wanted to be killed so there wouldn't be any further tortures. At some point, they made me an offer to stay there, to move to Shushi.

I was surprised, as Shushi had never been mentioned in the peace negotiations, and here they were telling me they had even occupied Shushi. They went so far as to offer me a move to a third country, to renounce my citizenship and get a job abroad. I said I'd go along with that; I just wanted to get out of the place. I figured that as soon as I had the prison gate behind me, I was sure I could make it back to Armenia. I was so exhausted from crying every day my T-shirt was wet through, soaked with tears, but I wouldn't stop crying.

Hearing him speak, I wondered whether an Azeri would have a sliver of empathy for the Armenians slaughtered in Sumgait[4] or could muster any understanding of an Armenian's pain or hatred of them from the massacres that happened before Khojaly. Of course, I'm not seeking to justify any slaughter; but before any Azeri wishes to talk about Khojaly in 1992, he ought to acknowledge the killing of hundreds of Armenian civilians in Sumgait in 1988: people burned alive, women raped. Moreover, every Azeri ought to acknowledge the pogrom against Armenians in Azerbaijan's capital, Baku, in 1990[5] if the goal is to seriously and in good faith approach the historical events and mutual atrocities, and not merely nationalist propaganda and agitation.

Sadly, though, the Azeris haven't demonstrated a single step of reconciliation. On the contrary, they have taken many steps

---

[4] I intentionally chose a German article on the Sumgait massacre in the interests of neutrality and non-bias. Der Spiegel is a leading German magazine, both online and in print. The article title translates as "We are going to exterminate you [Armenians in Sumgait, Azerbaijan]: https://www.spiegel.de/politik/wir-werden-euch-ausrotten-a-99765f90-0002-0001-0000-000013687666

[5] Recognition of the victims of the Baku and Sumgait pogroms: https://www.congress.gov/congressional-record/2020/01/30/extensions-of-remarks-section/article/E112-3

(and still are: it is known as "caviar diplomacy")[6] to cover up their crimes. The Armenian nation has often undergone ethnic cleansing throughout its history, yet here are Armenians seeking to understand the perpetrators' pain. The situation couldn't be more cynical.

> In the end, they stopped asking me their questions, as they had got it through their heads that I was an ordinary herdsman who knew a lot about cattle and nothing about the military. They had information about Armenian military bases that I'd never heard of. Thus, on November 9th, they told me that the war was over and that Armenian and Azeri soldiers would live peacefully together. They had nothing more to fight for, as they had already taken what was rightfully theirs. I was overjoyed that the war was over. I didn't care about the lost lands; let these lowlifes take whatever belonged to them. I cared more about the young conscripts who had been joining the army and had very little chance of returning home. I had no idea what to think."
>
> It was December 8th when the phone rang right in front of my cell door. Every time someone called that number, it meant they were getting an order either to torture me or to take me to another cell to meet someone. Even when the prison governor went home, he would call from home and tell the guards to beat me so hard that he could hear my screams down the phone. Anyway, the order that came down the phone this time was for the guards to give me a haircut and make sure I looked healthy. A week later, on December 14th, they

[6] The Economist, "Caviar Diplomacy in Azerbaijan": https://www.economist.com/1843/2016/08/31/caviar-diplomacy-in-azerbaijan

gave me a bar of soap for the first time ever, and I had the chance to take a shower. Then, the guard told me that I was going to be taken out to a square to be shot at dawn.

The next morning, I was expecting that fate. One of the generals came into my cell and made me strip. Then he gave me new clothes and left. I asked the guard again what awaited me, and he said they would soon kill me. I was silently praying that they'd shoot me cleanly without torturing me first. I was taken to the prison hospital for a chest X-ray and some blood tests. Then, as I left the hospital, the guards gave me my own clothes and the letters the Red Cross had brought for me. I saw two scenarios in my mind: either the Azeris would kill me, or they would give me the chance to return to Armenia. The suspense was getting more and more unbearable as they were driving me from one place to another. I just wanted them to finish it off.

We reached their position on the Armenian border, and they removed my blindfold. When I saw their troops in front of me, I thought they were going to mow me down then and there. But instead, one of the officers pointed to the Armenian border and told me I would soon be seeing my children again. We started walking. As we got closer to the people waiting on the other side, I realized they were Armenians. I'd always imagined that the Armenians would be waiting with some captives of their own to exchange for their prisoners held in Azerbaijan—but I was the only captive handed over to Armenia that day. They signed some document, and I was left standing there with the same numbness that had paralyzed me on the first day of captivity. I always dreamt of touching the soil in front of my house again. As I crossed the Armenian border, I couldn't contain myself any longer; I threw myself on

the ground and hugged it. I touched and smelt it. I felt
I was home.

Narek showed me the clothes he'd brought with him from captivity. Whatever item he took out of a bag, it jogged memories.
One of the sweaters was blood-sodden from a memorable beating in the old KGB[7] building. Everything he took out of the bags
was made in Turkey. He took out a T-shirt with "Istanbul" printed on it. There were only two or three garments in each bag.

> I would wear two pairs of socks, not only because of
> the cold, but because it would protect my foot wounds
> from trailing over the floor. I wouldn't want anyone to
> undergo the experiences I had there. It was a miracle
> I left the cell alive. I always prayed that at least they
> would give my corpse back to Armenia. I was scared
> they would just toss my body into a skip, and then I
> realized it was meaningless even to think about that,
> because if I was dead, what would I care where my
> body ended up? Then I imagined my grave and faced
> questions I never thought I would face.
>
> During those 161 days, I reflected a lot on my life.
> I thought about my relationships with people, those
> I'd wronged, those I wished to apologize to, the way I'd
> talked to some people. I was also apprehensive about
> coming home, as I had no idea how society would wel-
> come me. I thought maybe people would call me a trai-
> tor or make light of me. But there was an amicable
> welcome for me even at the Armenian border. We sat
> down and ate together. I had the chance to eat food

---

[7] In the Soviet Union, the KGB's responsibilities included the protection of the
political leadership, the supervision of border guards, and general surveillance
of the people: https://www.thoughtco.com/history-of-the-kgb-4148458

again. What I'd longed for most was condensed milk. Every time the Azeri soldiers drank tea with baklava, they would have that on the table. I promised myself I would eat everything up to the last morsel and never throw food away.

What is your message to the world?

I would love to thank the Red Cross.

He took a moment to reflect on his answer and went on:

No matter what might happen, people should always have hope. Nothing would happen without a cause, I realized, so it was important to resist. Some people end their lives when they feel out of their depth; I thought that was the cowardliest step one could take. But some people do kill themselves, without giving a second thought to their family. I had endured every humiliation. They would throw me on the ground and throttle me, and I felt everything go through me; I had every reason to kill myself. If I came across an Azeri, I might deal him a couple of slaps, but I would never do the same to them that they did to me. I wouldn't just hate every Azeri or Turk because of some idiots treating me like trash.

If the Armenians had won the war, do you think you would still be alive?

No. I was sure the Azeris were going to tear me limb from limb if that had been the outcome. I also felt wretched because I couldn't do anything for my country. I felt like a dog in that cell. The days when the Armenians gained ground were the worst days for me.

They wouldn't let me eat or drink anything. Imagine you'd hunted an animal—a wolf—and put him in a cage. And then imagine the locals from the village were intrigued and came to have a gawp at the beast. That's what I was to them. I was caged, and everyone passing by would come into my cell. I had at least ten people a day calling in on me, and they would punch me in the face or try out new things. The difference between me and a dog was that a dog could at least bark or bite back. I had to stand there and let them have their way. I couldn't sit down; as soon as I tried to, they would start the humiliations again. Awful people. Nothing human about them.

Every time the Azeri army took new territory during the war, the prison officers would lay the table and celebrate. Once, they ate a banana and threw the peel in front of me, like a dog. I was even happy with that. At that moment, if they'd let me, I'd have started rooting through the trash, like the homeless people I used to ignore on the streets. Hunger is the worst thing that can ever happen to anyone. I thought of the three children in my village whose parents had abandoned them. I was an adult, and I couldn't handle this hunger; how did those kids cope? I endured everything during those six months.

I'm fortunate they didn't hit me on my head much; that is why my memory hasn't been affected. Twenty of them would start beating me; all I longed for then was a deadly blow. Maybe if I'd stayed in for ten more days, they'd have whacked me somewhere very sensitive, and I would have lost my mind. The last ten days, they calmed down; I wondered what was happening. Of the whole six months, only the last ten days were relaxed. I wasn't used to it.

He showed me the wounds on his feet, the scars of electric shocks.

> I always dreamt they were going to take me out and force me to labor all day, but I hated it when they touched me. I felt I was the worst criminal in the entire world, in a dark, isolated, damp cell.

Additionally, there was his letter on the table. He hadn't known in prison what he was allowed to say in a letter or that it would even reach his family, so he'd been concise the first time: "Hello everyone, I love you all. I am well; everything is fine with me. Take care. Sending you kisses."

The second letter was longer and more detailed: "Hi, Hermine [Narek's wife], how are you and the children? I really want to come home. I think maybe the government can exchange me for the two Azeri prisoners[8] held in Armenia. I think if they want to, they can save my life at that price. I don't know what will happen to me. My warm greetings to everyone. I am sending you and the kids lots of kisses and hugs. Hermine, please buy a bike for Gor [Narek and Hermine's son] and tell him it's from me."

He wrote this letter on September 23rd. No matter how much Hermine wanted her husband to come back home, she thought that what Narek was asking was nonsense, an impossibility.

> I wanted to go and visit the parents of the young man killed by these two terrorists and was willing to try, but I knew it was useless. I also stopped taking part in the protests and focused on working with the Red Cross and lawyers instead. The Armenian Government

---

[8] The Tsakanian family's story is told in Chapter 11: All in Exchange for All.

couldn't do anything, it was all dependent on Smbat Tsakanian's family, but I couldn't look them in the eye and ask them to give their blessing to setting their son's murderers free.

Hermine, Narek's wife, was one of the strongest women I talked to. Usually, the family is the worst affected in cases like Narek's, and people rally around them. Yet Hermine took charge of the situation and assured everyone that Narek would be coming back. She went out with a party of men to search the nearby fields for her husband. She started a campaign on Facebook and went out to protest for her husband's return. She contacted the International Committee of the Red Cross Delegation and the Human Rights Ombudsman's Office in Armenia and pressed the Armenian authorities to take responsibility for her husband. An Armenian police officer even told her that the police had convinced themselves Narek must have turned his phone off to have a dalliance with another woman. Hermine made them go out and look for him, even if he was with another woman.

Hermine never gave up hope. On the contrary, she was sure Narek would return, and that made Narek stronger.

CHAPTER 2

Through Thick and Thin

This time, I traveled to Stepanakert, the capital of Artsakh (Nagorno-Karabakh), to interview some detainees subjected to torture and cruelty. Arega, a 72-year-old (!) woman from Avetaranots, who had suffered a stroke, was captured from her house along with her husband. She couldn't stop crying during the whole interview. Her left arm was shaking like a leaf, trembling with fear from the awakened memories.

Her daughter, Gohar, constantly interrupted and answered on her behalf because Arega was getting too emotional most of the time. She would start crying and trembling. We took many breaks. It was one of the most harrowing interviews I conducted during the whole month of March.

> I woke up to make a fire in the stove, and someone entered the living room. I told my husband that someone had just run into the house. He stood up to look, and at once, lots of soldiers entered the room and started talking Azeri. I panicked and started crying. They all had weapons, daggers pointed at us, and were screaming and threatening. They approached my husband, twisted his arms behind his back, and led him out of the room. I started crying, shouting for help, but no one was in the village, as they'd all fled to Stepanakert. They pushed me as I was resisting, but they forced me out. They didn't even let me pack any warm clothes.

Why hadn't you, too, fled the village?

I actually did ask my husband if we should leave together, but he refused. He could not believe the Azeris
would ever enter the village and told me to be calm
and stay with him. As the Azeris entered the house,
they opened all the cupboards, searched for items under the beds, and turned the place into chaos. I wanted to restore order to our possessions, but they intervened and wouldn't let me. At some point, an Azeri
pointed to his golden necklace and asked if we had any.
I could somehow make him understand that we didn't
have any gold at home. He got so angry that he pulled
my daughter's portrait off the wall and threw it out.
Afterward, they commanded us to stand up and leave
the house while pointing a gun at us.

As they led us out of our house, they started
talking with my husband. His name was Edik [the familiar form of Edvard], and he could speak Azeri. He
was going to talk with them, answer, and I would fear
that it would make them even angrier. I asked Edik to
stop answering them. But it was in vain. After some
time, we were told to walk up the hill. I'm 72, and my
legs were too weak to cope with that. My heart felt
heavy, I was running out of breath, but I had to keep
walking. Whenever I paused for a second, they would
jab a rifle butt into my back and make me carry on up
the hill. Halfway up, I fell over, and that made them
wait. So they got more aggressive, made me stand back
up, and started pushing me harder to walk further.

I was almost ready to believe that these people were genuinely
kind-hearted and that it was just me who'd got the wrong end of
the stick and was trying to convince the readers to the contrary.
I wondered if those Azeri soldiers reckoned they could make a
name for themselves by making a 72-year-old grandma cry. They
must be very proud of themselves.

They took us to our neighbor Kolya's house. There was no one inside except some more Azeri soldiers. They told my husband and me to sit on the floor and wait. After some time, the Azeri soldiers brought another Armenian in. He was covered in blood, and his clothes were all torn apart; his knees were bleeding. Girish—his real name is Setrak, but people in the village named him Girish—was also in his seventies, nearly blind, and he was crying continually. As we got to Kolya's place, we saw the Azeris had lit a fire in the garden, prepared to gather for dinner, and were drinking and enjoying themselves. After several hours, they took us to another abandoned house in the village and threw us into the shed.

Shortly afterward, they opened the door. Another neighbor of ours, Baghdasar, was also captured and joined us in the shed. Baghdasar told us he was determined to find a way to run away. That night, we stayed in the cowshed, soaked to the bone and sodden in manure. Baghdasar was thinking of ways to get out of there and run away. And so he did. He managed to dislodge one of the stones from the wall, which was already unstable, and he ran away, telling my husband and Girish not to say anything to the Azeri soldiers. We were starving and parched, but none of them would give us anything to eat or drink. The cold penetrated my bones. My husband and Girish fell asleep, but I couldn't. I was too scared, crying, and shivering.

As the Azeris checked on us, they saw that there were only three of us instead of four. The Azeri soldiers thought I must have helped Baghdasar because my husband and Girish were sleeping. I was trembling and crying the whole time. I was so sure they would kill me right that moment. My husband wasn't saying anything, and they started beating him up. Eventually, he told them of some possible places Baghdasar might have gone to. However, their search was in vain.

As we were waiting for a car to take us to the nearby mountains, some Azeri soldiers punched Edik several times and kicked him with booted feet. My husband was unshaven because we didn't have any razors at home, and his hands were also trembling. He looked like a soldier. The Azeris thought he must be involved in the war and told him they would kill him, yelling at him that at least he must have taken part in the first war in the 1990s. I was screaming and crying as I watched my husband being beaten. Finally, some soldiers stopped the beating. Then a car appeared, and they told us to get in. So we did, and we headed in the direction of a field strewn with timber.

They started talking to my husband again while some of them were loading up the big trucks with wood. They tied my husband's and Girish's hands and started beating them up. Once they were satisfied, we were commanded to sit on the top of the logs. We clambered on top of them in a big truck and left the place behind us. We drove for many hours: hungry, thirsty, cold, and unsure of what to expect. I asked where we were, and they told me we were in Baku.

With a sob, Arega murmured: "Baku, I wish it were burnt down. Everyone there should be burned."

It was the third day of captivity. We hadn't eaten and drunk anything. In Baku, they took us to an abandoned house. My husband wanted to go to the toilet, and so did Girish, but they just did it in the room, as the doors were locked. The following day, the Azeris came back and started beating the men for having relieved themselves in that room. I started crying and screaming again. After some time, they brought us to Baku Prison. Right at the entrance, I was separated from my husband and Girish. That was the last time I saw my husband alive.

As I entered the cell, I started crying and yelling. I didn't know what was happening, but I felt so lonely and sad. There was already another woman in the cell. She came closer to me and tried to calm me down. "God, why I should have to go through this nightmare," I was repeating while crying continually. Arineh[9] saved my life. It was freezing inside the cell, and the heating was not working at all. We started sleeping in one bed to warm each other and help each other survive the cold. But still, it was unbearable. Each day was the same. We were so hurt: whenever we cried, the guards would start laughing at us. As Arineh was more experienced in captivity, she was taking the situation more in her stride. One day, I got her to ask one of the guards about my husband. Since we'd been separated that day, I hadn't heard anything more about him. And one day, as I tried to ask the same question, Arineh told me that my husband had died and that we had the opportunity to go and bid him farewell.

Did he die, or was he killed?

I don't know. Edvard was like a shriveled piece of meat, looking totally drained and tortured when I saw his body. I asked what had happened, and the Azeri officers told me he had "had a heart attack." But I could see black bruises all over his body. They killed him.

---

[9] This woman wanted to stay anonymous, so I gave her the pseudonym Arineh.

> They beat him to death. They never beat Arineh or me,
> but they killed my husband.

Arega was traumatized from captivity and couldn't remember much about going to view her husband's body, but she clearly described his face as being black and blue. However, Arega's daughter, Gohar, mentioned that her father had been an asthmatic and was on medication. Unfortunately, in captivity, he was unable to take any medicine.

> When Dad died, the Red Cross in Baku called us to tell
> us the news.

So the Azeri authorities repatriated Edvard's body on December 28, 2020. The Armenian authorities issued his death certificate, giving the cause of death as blunt-object brain trauma, cerebral swelling, and acute disorder of vital brain functions. His body arrived in Yerevan on January 3rd, and the next day the family buried him.

Do you remember the day you were freed, Arega?

> A guard opened the door and told me the news. Arineh
> helped me put my clothes on. But as I was taken out
> of the cell, the Azeri guards took all of my clothes off.
> I had to stand naked in front of these men because
> they wanted to be sure that I wasn't taking anything
> with me to Armenia. After they were sure I had noth-
> ing with me, I sat in the car to the airport. On the way,
> they kept me handcuffed. I was so thirsty; I was asking
> for water. But no one cared. Then Girish and Jonik,
> also from my village, joined me at the airport. Unfor-
> tunately, I had to leave Arineh behind.
> I had never seen an airplane in my life, and there
> one was, waiting to bring me home. Onboard, I saw a

corpse covered with a white sheet. I thought it might be my husband, but I didn't dare to take a look. Then, as we arrived in Yerevan, I started crying again. No one came to pick me up, and I felt utterly abandoned. My children were not there.

The last sentence hurt Gohar's feelings, so she reacted immediately.

We didn't know she was returning that day. We had no idea.

The next day, the Armenian officers showed Arega a corpse for her to identify whether it was Edvard's. It was not; it was a younger man with a scar on his face. When the family announced that the body was not Edvard's, the Azeri authorities denied having sent the wrong body. However, on December 28th, they corrected their mistake by dispatching Edvard's body to Yerevan.

As Gohar was also participating in the conversation, she wanted me to know that she had tried to get her parents out of the village before the invasion.

We went so many times to get them out of the village, but Dad was very stubborn, and he wouldn't accept that the Azeris might reach Avetaranots. On October 22nd or 23rd, there was a bus to take everyone out of the village. Some people did go, and they urged my parents to get their stuff together and leave with the rest. Dad wouldn't listen, and Mum stayed by his side. Vladik [Gohar's husband] went back again on October 27th to convince Dad, but he refused again. That day, I called Vladik and told him that the Azeris had already entered the village. He immediately called Dad back to talk to him for the last time, and an Azeri soldier answered the phone.

Vladik was also in the room during the last part of the interview. He took up the story:

> "I talked to the guy in Azeri. I just asked the soldier where he was, and he said he was in Azerbaijan. I immediately understood they had captured Arega and Edik. It was too late. On November 3rd, we had a phone call from the Red Cross, and they confirmed my parents had been captured. So we went to the Red Cross and wrote a letter to Arega assuring her we would do everything we could to get them back. We even wanted to buy some medicine to send for them both. A few days later, the Red Cross called us and told us that they both were doing well and sent their warmest greetings. They even said the letter had already arrived. Yet when Arega returned, she said she hadn't had any letter."

The outcome: Edik died, or maybe he was killed. We will never know the truth. Arega was left in Stepanakert, living with her daughter; Baghdasar managed to escape and also settled in Stepanakert. The day he escaped, he hid in a tandoor oven at his sister's house; as dusk fell, he fled to Stepanakert. Jonik, who was on the repatriation flight with Arega, arrived in Yerevan and died a matter of days later. Of Girish's fate, nothing is known.

CHAPTER 3

The Birthday "Gift" She Will Never Forget

The atmosphere in this very narrow room in the center of Stepanakert was unpleasant. Sasha's wife was insisting he was 71 years old; Sasha was absolutely sure he was still 70. It was getting nasty, as Sasha was very intolerant and was raising his voice, telling his wife to shut up. He was born in a village called Khrmanjugh. After getting married, he took his family to Hadrut, in the south-eastern corner of Artsakh, to ensure a better life for his children, as the city offered more options. He worked as a driver and was drafted into the Red Army in 1969. After finishing military service, Sasha went back to living and working as a driver in Hadrut for the rest of his life.

> I fought in the first war between Armenia and Azerbaijan. During the latest war, I could do nothing, as I was too old to fight. We already knew the Azeris had taken Hadrut, and people had fled the area couple of days earlier. I couldn't follow them. Hearing noises in my house, I went to investigate and found 20 or 30 soldiers leveling their weapons at me."
>
> I could speak Azeri. As they pointed their guns at me, they commanded me not to make any moves to escape; otherwise, they would kill me. I said, "You want to kill me? Come on, then. Open the door and get on with it." One of the Azeris said that I'd left a good impression on him, but it wouldn't do any good, as they had orders that by November 1st, there were to be no Armenians left in Hadrut.

Like Edvard (Arega's husband), Sasha simply didn't believe the Azeri soldiers could ever enter the city; but he didn't want to leave his home, either. Knowing his father's stance, Sasha's 44-year-old son, Arsen, couldn't leave him behind. On October 10th, Azeri soldiers took control of Hadrut. Arsen's place was in the city center. He rushed home to convince his dad to leave. But there was no time. As Arsen entered the house, the Azeri soldiers were already there talking to his dad. Sasha could do nothing but desperately watch the Azeri soldiers tying Arsen's hands behind his back and taking him away.

> After a while, they led me away from my home. We did not quarrel; I did whatever they told me to do, and everything seemed to be fine at the outset. I wasn't blindfolded; the soldiers took me somewhere in Hadrut and joined the rest of their company. It was getting dark outside, and they set the table to have dinner. I was allowed to join them; we drank vodka together. After dinner, I asked them if I could go; but I knew it was a stupid question. So off we headed to join another group of Azeri soldiers. As we arrived, someone approached me and told me, "You killed my brother." I was shocked. I started negotiating and trying to persuade him that what he was saying was impossible. However, he was very convinced and didn't want to waste his time. He took a stone from the car and crushed it against my fingers, pushed me, kicked me, and poked me with a sharp metal rod.

Sasha showed the scars on his hands. His left foot was also covered in bruises and scars, as the Azeris had bent his legs around a metal bar and hung him upside down from a tree. Then the Azeri soldiers started beating him with a rifle butt. Finally, when their thirst for torture was satisfied, they untied his legs and let him drop to the ground. What happened next was one of the most crucial parts of Sasha's story.

While I was still distraught from the pain, a car came
and parked next to us. Around six or seven Armenian captives walked toward me. One of them was my
son, Arsen. I couldn't believe I was seeing him again.
I started screaming at them that he was my son and
begging them to stop the torture. One of them took
a massive stone and hit him with it; I jumped, yelled,
and tried to do everything to save my son from the un-
ending beatings. The pain was endless. After beatings
and harassment, we were put into a car and taken to an
abandoned place in Hadrut.

Sasha and Arsen were taken to the same place. However, they
only could exchange a few words in the car. After that, they met
again in Baku but had no chance to talk to each other.

I had word that Arsen was in the same building as me.
The interrogator's last name was Hadjiev. I begged
him to give me one chance to meet my son, but it was
in vain. He said it might be dangerous, not only for me
but even for him. It was such a pain to know my son
was in the same building as I, but I could do nothing
even to see him for two minutes. We both were still in
Hadrut.

Marineh, Sasha's daughter, was also in the room during our interview. The last phone call she had with her brother was on
October 9th. A month later, on November 9th, a video circulating
on social media showed Azeri soldiers forcing Sasha to kiss the
Azeri flag and repeat the slogan "Karabakh is Azerbaijan." At
least the family knew he was alive; they still had no news of Arsen, though.

I was thrown on the floor as some specialist soldiers
entered the room. Luckily, I spoke their language well

enough to answer their questions, and they also spoke pretty good Armenian. One of them wanted to shoot me, but some of the others prevented him. Maybe it was my knowledge of the Azeri language that saved my life. After several hours, I and the other six or seven Armenian captives were taken to Baku. Unfortunately, Arsen and I were in separate cars. If only I'd been with him in the same car.

That day, they were taken to Baku. In Baku Prison, Sasha saw Arsen again. Unfortunately, they had no chance to talk, but at least Sasha knew Arsen was in the same facility as he was. He asked the guards to arrange a meeting with him, but it proved to be too late.

I was kept in prison for two months. I wouldn't want to complain or exaggerate. Once I was in the cell, there was no further torture, at least in my case. The food was never sufficient, but we did get three meals a day. The Azeri officers also tried to convince me to stay in the country. They even promised me they would bring my family over to Baku. But it was not an option for me. They liked me a lot. Even when I met the Red Cross, the Azeri officers would tell me during the meeting how well-behaved I was. I told the Red Cross that I wasn't being beaten, although they could see my fingers had bruises and my legs were injured. I didn't tell them anything.

As noted in one of our other stories, Sasha was in the same cell as Samvel A., Ruben, and Narek. According to Samvel, Sasha behaved very oddly in the cell, as if he had psychological issues. However, when I asked Sasha about his cellmates, he couldn't remember their names. Sasha returned home on December 14, 2020 among the first group of 44 Armenian POWs and civilians and was admitted to Erebuni Medical Center. When the doctors examined him, they found Sasha's wrists were broken, and his ankle was deeply scarred from being tightly bound with wire. The doctors also found traces of carbon monoxide in his lungs, but Sasha couldn't remember anything that might explain that. X-ray results indicated that his nose had been broken and his left rib severely fractured. At the hospital, Sasha was disoriented and asked a lot about his son. However, at that time, no one had news of Arsen.

Arsen's sister, Marine, who was fighting for her father's and brother's rights, intervened in our conversation.

On October 11, 2020, Hadrut was overrun by Azeri soldiers, and we already knew Arsen and Dad had been captured. Arsen actually lived in Russia; he was just on a visit to us at the time and had been due to leave again on October 1st. As the war between Armenia and Azerbaijan broke out at that time, he joined the local militia instead and went off to fight. His friends said that when Arsen found out that the Azeris were in Hadrut, he went to help his dad get out of the town, but he couldn't manage to do it.

As we had no news of either of them, I turned to the Red Cross and the Human Rights Ombudsman's Office in Yerevan. I told them that there were two missing persons from a single family. We had no news of them for a month. On November 14th, I saw a video of my dad on Facebook. Although he had different clothes on, I recognized him. I showed the video to the Red Cross and to the Human Rights Ombudsmen of both Artsakh and Armenia. I also went to see the Russian peacekeeping general, Muradov, and showed him the video. When my dad returned on December 14th, he spoke of Arsen also being in Baku. Only then could I start fighting for Arsen's life as well

On January 6th—my mother's birthday—Azeri soldiers made a video of my brother and uploaded it to TikTok. In it, they were talking to Arsen at the police station in Hadrut. Arsen was a very handsome man, but in the video, one could barely recognize him. He was being very aggressive and still resisting. On the other hand, in the second video, released on January 8th, Arsen looked cowed. He had a long beard, which had gone completely white. Mockingly, the Azeri soldiers were telling him to "Say hello to Shusha." (This flagship town, known as Shushi in Armenian, was unexpectedly occupied by the Azeris during the last war in 2020.)

Arsen's mother showed me a picture of him where he looked completely different from the man seen in the video. In the video, Arsen looked tortured, exhausted, and was ordered to say, "Azeris are good people," "Pashinyan götveran,"[10] and other degrading expressions. It was hard to see Arsen's mother, Aida, mourning his son's death. She kept repeating: "Look, this was the day when he was taken to be killed." And the sister told me, "This was the last video of him." They were both sure of it: in the last video, Arsen was being led off to be shot.

Marineh, Arsen's sister, shared more pictures and gave consent for them to be published. I wanted to publish only one. It is, for me, too brutal to share all of them with the public. The portrait on the left is Arsen before enduring his dreadful torture. On the right, we can see the true face of Azerbaijan and the level of naivety of some Armenians who believe there is hope these two nations can peacefully coexist.

---

[10] Turkish for "The Armenian Prime Minister is a scumbag."

On January 13, 2021, the ECtHR asked Azerbaijan to provide information about Arsen's situation.[11] Just five days later, in a search for dead bodies around Hadrut, assisted by Russian peacekeepers and the Red Cross, Arsen's body was found near the village of Aygestan. The mortuary doctor told Arsen's family that he had been killed on January 15th. The family was informed of his death on January 19th. Marineh showed me a video of Arsen's body. The left side of his body was heavily tortured, two gunshot wounds were seen in the middle of his forehead, and his left armpit had been burned. The attractive young Arsen I saw in the portrait was barely comparable to the person he had become in the enemy's hands.

The mourning sounds of Arsen's mother's still ring in my ears. She was not loud, but the ache she expressed could never be forgotten.

Marineh continued.

When my son and I went to identify Arsen's body, we found his body was filthy, and there was sand all over him. They killed him in Hadrut, excavated a hole, put his body in it, and filled it in. But they left his head sticking out, so the search party was able to spot him and exhume his body. The search party took his body to the morgue in Stepanakert. On his birthday, on January 20th, it was Arsen's funeral. The Azeris are fond of symbolism: on my mother's birthday, they posted the video; on Arsen's birthday, we buried him.

---

[11] Another very interesting article connected to Sasha's and Arega's story, written by Tanya Lokshina, March 2021: *Survivors of Unlawful Detention in Nagorno-Karabakh Speak out about War Crimes.* Online at: https://www.hrw.org/node/378197/printable/print

CHAPTER 4

A Story of Two Friends

People often asked me how I managed to reach the former Armenian POWs and civilians to interview them. Of course, before coming to Armenia, I already had a list of former Armenian captives and had gotten in touch with some of them. Unbelievably, though, after nearly every interview, I had contact details for new people. The next two interviewees weren't on my list before I traveled to Artsakh. In Stepanakert, I met the current Human Rights Ombudsman of Artsakh, Gegham Stepanyan. Through him, I was able to interview Ramiz and Abel, who were, fortunately, in captivity for only five days; however, five days were quite enough for them.

> The sun was already going down. We wanted to check the one-hectare field we both owned before the rainy season began. It was November 28th when Abel and I headed to the field to look it over and calculate the cultivation costs.

Abel, a childhood friend of Ramiz, was a tractor driver. As Ramiz had severe back problems, Abel helped him with some of his farming tasks. Abel was 53 years old, and Ramiz was 47. Both were from Khramort, a village in the district of Askeran. The case now narrated happened after the ceasefire agreement between Armenia and Azerbaijan.

> As we were approaching the field, we realized the road was too rocky, and it could easily wreck my car [an Opel]. So I asked Abel to try to bypass that rough stretch. As soon as we turned the steering wheel, Azeri soldiers blocked us in.

Does this mean you inadvertently crossed their border while skirting around the rocky patch of road?

> No, they had crossed the border and entered about 150 meters into our territory. We told them that the field was ours. They answered: "You have no lands in Artsakh; all you have is in Armenia. So you should already have moved there."

At that time, there were still around 30 Armenian families living in the village of Khramort. Azerbaijan did not occupy Khramort: this troop of Azeri soldiers had just seized the opportunity of dusk, entered the field, and captured both Abel and Ramiz.

> The Azeri soldiers pointed a gun at us and told us to get out of the car. They pressed our bodies against the ground. We wanted to negotiate and told them we hadn't crossed any border. If so, where were the signs about the border or about the area belonging to them? We hadn't crossed any border. Abel did his best to clarify that no sign was warning people of a border. They took our mobile phones and started dragging us back and forth. There were around 30 soldiers wearing their uniforms, their faces covered with balaclavas. We tried to talk to them, told them we were civilians and were coming to check on our fields. We even promised them we would not come back anymore; we just wanted to negotiate and find a compromise with them. It didn't get us anywhere. Suddenly, two cars parked right next to us. Some trained men covered our faces, handcuffed us, and told us they would take us to their general but that we would be back home again the next day.
>
> They also drove my car behind us. We were taken either to Tigranakert or to Maragha. It took us only 20 to 25 minutes. When we arrived, they became ex-

tremely aggressive. The room was almost empty; it
was either an abandoned school or some official building or other. Actually, the chairs we saw, later on, were
for pupils, so it must have been a school. We were
each made to sit on a chair, our hands were tied to
the chairs, and we faced each other across two corners
of the room. We couldn't talk, and neither could we
sleep. The whole night, we were savagely beaten. They
took an iron rod and bashed Abel on the head. In the
end, I couldn't even make out what they were using to
torture us. Our hands were so tightly cuffed that we
could do nothing to shield ourselves. At some point,
they took us to a different room. As we were blindfolded, we couldn't see which direction we had to walk in.
Several times, we hit the wall or fell.

Abel was sure they were in Maragha. He said he'd spotted a
Christmas tree in front of the building. The toilet was outside,
and a huge generator was still humming near the building.

Next morning, on November 29th, around six men carried us to another car. We headed to Baku. On the way,
they started making fun of us. We had masks on, and
we had to say 'Karabakh is Azerbaijan' constantly. They
were so stupid that they were filming us with our Covid
masks on. But the longer we drove, the more aggressive
they became. They were cursing not only us but our
mothers and sisters. On the border between Azerbaijan and Artsakh, we waited half an hour for the traffic
police car to arrive. I saw the Azeri livery on the car:
Yol Polisi. We stayed sitting in the back of the car, and
after a while, we arrived in the city of Barda. I caught
glimpses of the city from beneath my blindfold. Some-
time later, they delivered us to their military police station, took us out of the car, and dragged us to a cell.

Both Abel and Ramiz could speak Azeri. During the interrogation, Ramiz did most of the talking. Abel only intervened when he had something essential to share that Ramiz had omitted to mention.

> After an hour, two very highly-trained soldiers entered the cell. Initially, we tried to talk to them. We told them that the war was over, and we hadn't even fought in it. We were just wanting to visit our fields, where we grow our food. A peace accord had been signed, we added. But they were both deeply convinced we had killed their people during the first war in the 1990s.

Of course, I stopped Ramiz right there and helped him understand that we did not, in fact, have a single peace accord with Azerbaijan. It was merely a ceasefire agreement. For me, it was essential to use the opportunity to point out one more time that the war was not over at all and that the deal in place when this incident happened had been a ceasefire and not a peace treaty.
Abel continued.

> The day we were captured, I had a warm coat from old army supplies and a sweater on. Having something connected to the Armenian army made my condition worse in prison. I told them I only had it on because it was a warm garment; however, it made them believe we were rangers and had crossed the border for some military operation. They quickly became enraged. I was tortured more than Ramiz, as they couldn't bear the sight of an Armenian military uniform.

Abel was more hotheaded; Ramiz ultimately turned out to be the opposite: calm, with a tranquil facial expression.

> Also, because I was older than Ramiz, my age was consistent with their calculations of my having taken part in the first war. They were convinced I'd also been at

Khojaly back at the time of the massacre. They interrogated me exclusively on that topic, asking me where I'd been then, how many people I'd killed, and who my commanders were. The focus was only on Khojaly. They told me that I was supposed to give a recorded interview, during which I would have to say that Vitali Balasanyan, Seyran Ohanyan, and Arkadi Ter-Tadevosyan had ordered us to enter Khojaly with 1,000 to 1,500 soldiers and to slaughter everyone. I told them I wasn't there; I was in Russia back then and didn't fight in that war. My answer was a huge mistake. They lost their cool and started humiliating me. I asked them to give me three days to reflect. They gave me two days to think about recording the interview; luckily, we were moved to another prison after two days.

Most of the time, I was tortured because of my stubborn character. I told the Azeri officers that it was them who started the war in the 1990s: "You entered our village, and you set it on fire. People in our village had to flee a mountaintop for a year and a half, and you lived in our village of Khramort," I said to them, "and then we fought back and took our village back." They didn't like that for an answer, and they would just torture me. I also told them that I was a captive, that I had no power against them. And how weak they all must be, that they used this opportunity to torture me! They told me they would slaughter me and send my body parts through Baku.

First, Abel and Ramiz were both held in Barda. Then, when one of the commanders mentioned during an overheard phone call that he was going to Baku in a couple of hours, the Armenians understood they would be taken to Baku Prison next. So at midnight, they were put in a military police car and driven off to Azerbaijan's capital. It was raining outside. Inside the car, there was dense cigarette smoke and incessant dirty talk about Armenians.

> After six to seven hours, we arrived. Before we even managed to step out of the car, an Azeri soldier saw Abel's military jacket and started beating him. We tried to explain, to talk, but nothing helped. There was a loud Azeri mugham being sung outside the prison. We were separated after the first round of beatings. I was on the first floor, and Abel was one floor above me. The cells smelt terrible. There were bloodstains everywhere. It was not possible to stay mentally composed there. We constantly heard the voices of Armenians; at any moment, screams would cut through the silence. There was a woman, and her voice was the most awful for me. She would scream: "I've had nothing to eat, bring me food, open the door." She would repeat the same thing non-stop. Her voice stuck in my ears. She would moan from morning till night. I longed to die so that I didn't have to witness all this. We were tied up against the wall, with no chance to lie or sit down. Once, I asked them to loosen the bonds, as they were almost cutting my veins. They made them even tighter. We had no water to drink, no toilet to use, and of course, there was no question of food. All we did was stand there or have to endure the pain of beatings.

As Abel and Ramiz had been held in different cells, I also asked Abel to share his memories.

> I was severely humiliated during the night. On a single night, the Azeri soldiers entered the cell three to four times and started on us. The first time, they entered and told me to stand and to raise my left leg. After I did what I was ordered to do, the Azeri officer wanted

44

to know how I'd come to learn their language. I told them we learned it at school, but he was more convinced that I was an army ranger. I had a military coat, and I could speak their language. The next day, as I was being taken for interrogation, they broke three of my vertebrae. They struck me; I fell to the floor and hit my ear on the iron radiator. For a second, I thought my neck was broken, as I was bleeding. They brought some napkins and stopped the bleeding.

Ramiz continued:

The next day, they took me to the same floor as Abel, but we were in different cells. They opened the door, sat me opposite Abel, and started the interrogation. First, I had to answer a question about Abel's "participation in the Khojaly massacre." I said that he was in Russia at that time. The rest, you can imagine. After finishing their job, they opened the door, and they threw a third Armenian into the room to be interrogated along with us.

That man was Seyran, from Taghavart. He is still there now (January 2022). His son was killed during the last war in 2020. After his son's funeral in Yerevan, Seyran returned to visit his parents' grave in Taghavart. He was drunk as he drove back to Artsakh. Between two Russian peacekeeping positions, Azeri soldiers abducted him. Seyran was mourning his son's death, hadn't shaved, and was himself also in an Armenian military coat. The way Abel described him, he was naïve, couldn't speak much sense in any language at that moment, and was numb. The pain of burying his son had made him completely absent-minded.

The next morning, the Azeri soldiers took us to another interrogation room. There, they revealed another level of determination to torture us some more. They asked me again if Abel had participated in the war. I said no, and right away, iron rods hit my back, belly, and hands. I lost all sense of pain. All they wanted to hear from us was that we would "confess our participation in the war." They were sure we must have killed at least one Azeri. We were both lucky we could speak their language, as it helped us to communicate. But it also harmed us because they were sure we were special rangers sent by the army. Compared to Seyran, our knowledge of the language helped us more, as he was tortured most of the time because of his inability to communicate. When Seyran was interrogated, they would come and call either my name or Abel's to go and interpret for him.

We were severely tortured. On the way there, without any reason, they would just start beating us. Luckily, we were held in captivity for only five days. They didn't have time to subject us to electric shocks, but they did manage to make us taste death. They would start shouting: "We are coming; it is time to slaughter you." We knew the language, and we knew that they were intending to cart us off and kill us. However, the Azeri officers also made us the offer that we could stay in Azerbaijan, and they would send a special military unit to safeguard our families. They also promised to guarantee our security if we "accepted responsibility" for the massacre at Khojaly.

Were you able to ask them if they would recognize the earlier pogrom in Sumgait for their part?

No. That could have been fatal. Most of the time, we were not permitted to talk. The Azeri officers would just say the things they deeply believed anyway and start the beatings. We were not always together, either. Every time they saw my army coat, they would become extremely aggressive. They even gave me Armenian army trousers and boots to make me look like a complete military man. Once, they came up with two photos of me during the first war. They showed me a portrait of Vitali Balasanyan and said he was my "classmate." I said that I didn't know him, as I was from Khramort and he was from somewhere else altogether. "Where are our 5,000 victims? Their bodies are missing to this day; where did you hide them?" The beatings would always follow their questions. They just wanted any information connected to Khojaly.

Ramiz continued:

Each minute, life and death were in the balance. Every time they came to the cell, it was one step closer to death. We are so lucky that we had to stay there only for five days. My sister heard of our capture in time, and she went directly to the Russian peacekeeping general, Muradov. He saved us. Once, they came and told us that they were going to take us out and kill us. They took us to a square, kept us there the whole day, made us lingeringly expect the moment of death, and took us back to our cell again. This time, though, we were taken to a very clean place. There was a huge picture of President Aliyev hanging in the corridor of the prison. The red carpet and the Azeri flag were the key decorations in the place. When we were taken to meet the Russian general, the police stopped the car and asked what was happening. The Azeri commander said that he was taking us to Muradov.

The police said: "Come on, just solve the problem now; kill them," and sized their last chance to hit me through the small window and then did the same to Abel. I felt that everyone hated us. These five days, we had eaten nothing. Unknown Azeris would breeze in and talk about their enjoyment of slaughtering us. We had no appetite to eat or to drink. We didn't have time either, as we were busy being humiliated. On the way to the airport, I thought we might not be in Baku after all, and yet we were heading there. I thought of many things, but not coming back home. When we saw General Muradov, we asked where we were going to be taken to. He told us to leave the nightmare behind us and get ready to be back home in a couple of hours. And indeed, in a matter of hours, in the middle of the night, we were already in Erebuni Airport, in Armenia.

After returning to your village and finding out that the Azeri soldiers are posted just yards away and could repeat the whole affair, what do you feel now?

"There is no guarantee of our security in this village. I don't even have a weapon to protect myself," said Ramiz.

The field Ramiz and Abel owned was still under their control. At the end of our conversation, they conquered their fears and went back there. Around 300 to 400 hectares, full of persimmon trees, had been left abandoned. The situation was out of hand; Azeri soldiers had numerous positions around Khramort. They took up post anywhere they wanted and entered the village at will; there was no one to stop them. The first military position on the Azeri border with Artsakh, was where Abel and Ramiz had been captured. The second one was right above the village. Between these two positions, there were no Armenian soldiers or Russian peacekeepers. There was not a speck of safety for Abel and Ramiz. They had felt what the enemy is capable of doing, and precisely that experience enhanced their fear. From their homes, they could hear the yelling of Azeri soldiers; even when the dogs were barking, they could both hear it from home.

CHAPTER 5

The Honest Woman and Her Little Heart

I reserved a quiet spot in downtown Yerevan for my conversation with Arineh.[12] Even on the phone, she seemed highly punctilious and uncompromising. However, I must admit that her character and story were so crucial that I was ready to meet any condition to interview her. I just hoped the meeting could go ahead. Arineh was overweight, apparently with major respiratory problems. Later on, I learned she had severe diabetes.

Offering her a seat in a luxurious café on Pushkin Street, I started setting up my recording devices for the interview. To me, this place was a terrible choice as the music was deafening, and the patrons were looking askance at the pair of us, as neither of us was wearing a proper outfit for this swanky venue. Not that any of this bothered Arineh. She refused to meet me in a quiet place and picked the café herself. She sat down, lit her first cigarette, and ordered food. At this moment, I understood she was a real character.

Arineh was an ethnic Armenian previously from Dushanbe, the capital of Tajikistan. On February 13, 1990, she moved to Armenia with her family as a refugee. Arineh's grandmother and aunt were Armenians living in Baku until 1987. From her story, I understood that as the Soviet Union was breaking up, the family had been displaced from Baku to distant Dushanbe and from Dushanbe to Armenia, specifically to Abaran. I could see the sweat trickling down Arineh's neck. She needed pauses

---

[12] This interviewee wished to remain anonymous. I have given her a pseudonym, which is an Armenian name meaning "valiant woman."

to catch her breath. Sometimes, I thought of stopping the conversation, as she would suddenly start coughing as if she was struggling to get enough air. Arineh had a slight Russian accent when she spoke Armenian. When her family had moved to Armenia, Arineh could only speak Russian. Already a teenager by then, she had to start learning Armenian and getting integrated into society. After completing the seventh year of primary school in Abaran, she transferred to a trade school to learn tailoring.

> The first time I had ran away from home was in 1992. I went to Artsakh because I wanted to do something for the war effort. I was only 15 years old at that time. As I was a big lass, people thought I must be old enough to join up. I somehow managed to convince the soldiers heading to Artsakh to take me with them. I told them I was from an orphanage, had just turned 18, and had no other place to go but my 'home in Artsakh'. As we entered the capital, Stepanakert, I saw some random collapsed house and turned on the waterworks, acting as if it was my home.

I knew she had a lot to share, but I hadn't been expecting the story to start like this. One of the questions I was interested in asking was the reason why a 15-year-old would want to fight in a war rather than hang out with her friends. Her answer shook me: "To guard our native land."

She intentionally paused to impress upon me the absurdity of my question.

> Since Dad hadn't been lucky enough to have a son, I felt obliged to shoulder the role of a boy in my family. As a child, I loved military life, and I was interested in weapons. I wanted to go off to the war.

Well, this was hard to swallow. Before long, I was positively glad she'd chosen this café because there, she wouldn't catch the sound of me cracking my knuckles. At first glance, Arineh seemed an in-your-face, wild woman. However, as she continued her story, I became convinced she had a bubbly personality. She indeed loved life and lightened the life of many.

> I was in Artsakh from September 1992 to March 1993. That was when I had to be evacuated to Yerevan, as I had a traumatic brain injury and shell fragments in me. I stayed in Yerevan for a week before heading out to Artsakh again. By the end of the war, I'd been almost in every theater of operations. Whenever the local soldiers or captains realized I was underage, they would send me back to "my home" in Stepanakert. I would just join a different squad and head back out. When the war ended in May 1994, I was already 18 years old. Between then and 1997, I was in Artsakh for six months, serving in the army, and then I returned to my family in Abaran. In Abaran, I went through nightmares of privation. The mid-90s were the worst years, not just for me but for many Armenians. Our country was barely surviving after so many years of war.
>
> When the border situation with Azerbaijan escalated into war in April 2016, I heard the news on TV. There was no doubt I had to join the soldiers, so I looked around for people intending to head to the front. Fortunately, I managed to get a group together and departed for Artsakh. After staying there for around 20 days, I returned to Abaran.

The waitress brought Arineh's order. I let her tuck in and sat back, observing the café patrons. It was so sweet to see them turned out in their prettiest frocks, intent on looking nice and smelling lovely. For a moment, I wanted to be one of these ladies who lunch, indulge in ice cream, and chat about nonsense. Arineh had also made some efforts to doll herself up, but her face was pale, and there were heavy bags under her eyes. Her life experiences were engraved on her face.

> September 27th was the most painful day in my life. I got to the Yerkrapah Union of Volunteers[13] in Yerevan. I told them to send me to the front with the volunteers. After several days of negotiations, we managed to reach Jabrayil on October 2nd. When we arrived, I was shocked to witness the panic among our soldiers. The enemy was bombarding us all over the place and destroying our surroundings. We could neither turn on the lights nor move, as the enemy was coordinating its shelling with observations.

What was the reason the soldiers were in a panic? I asked this deliberately to see whether she could confirm the rumors I had previously heard. On November 10, 2020, Armenia and Azerbaijan signed a ceasefire agreement, and there was much talk of how some of the Armenian commanders had abandoned their men on the battlefield and legged it. So as I spoke with Arineh, I was keen to know whether the panic she had felt in Jabrayil had anything to do with these rumors.

> The panic had set in because one of the officers had made off, yes. He left the soldiers all alone and fled. Our own commander, Romik, together with Manvel from the Arabo detachment and General Komitas, got

---

[13] Yerkrapah Volunteers' Union is the largest and most influential union of war veterans in Armenia, founded in 1993 by Vazgen Sargsyan. For more information, see: https://armenian.usc.edu/the-yerkrapah-union-of-volunteers-at-a-crossroads/

everything back under control again, regrouped the forces, and did his best to reinspire the soldiers. As we formed up, an army doctor came over and asked if anyone was up for becoming his assistant. They needed a nurse who could help them in the operating room. There were wounded soldiers all over the place and very few doctors to save their lives. I was not a qualified nurse, but I wasn't a dunce either, so I agreed to help him in Jabrayil.

So we started triaging the wounded. The serious cases were brought to our unit, where we would patch them up as best we could before transferring them to the hospital by ambulance. The more lightly injured soldiers were taken to another department. Some hours into this, I was already numb and had lost sensation in my body. I helped the wounded soldiers for around three days solid, and I had no time to sleep or eat. My legs and joints swelled up. I developed pneumonia and was running a very high temperature. Ashkhen, I had no time to think about myself, especially when I knew quick action by me could save one more soldier's life.

The tension had dissipated, and the lines of fear had melted away from Arineh's face. She seemed more at ease than at the beginning of our conversation. Her ability to help one more and then yet one more soldier at the hospital gave her a confidence boost. It made her wilder on the one hand and squeezed her little heart even more on the other.

I was overwhelmed. I kept wilting again and again from hunger. Sometimes, the soldiers would pop a sweet in my mouth to ensure my blood sugar didn't drop, as they knew I was a diabetic. Then, on October 5th, Azeri troops started bombarding us from every angle. Soon, we heard the torment of war. I realized we had to quit the place.

The weather was awful the day we left. It was obvious I would not make it to the top of the mountain by foot. I begged my commander to leave me behind in Jabrayil. He took me somewhere else, though, and I guess he thought it would be safer there. My commander showed me which road to head for; I met an Armenian squad on the way. Whether they too were lost, I don't know, but in any case, they sent me completely the wrong way. I could have gone with them, but I couldn't keep pace with their march. My weight was always a problem for me. Never mind that I had lots of experience from the previous wars, it was still my first time in Jabrayil, and I wasn't familiar with the lie of the land. As I was left behind my squad, I started looking for a way out on my own. I had no idea where I was or how I could get out of the blockade.

I kept on walking, and I saw some cars parked in front of the secret service building. I sat in one of them and tried to start the engine. It just happens so easily in movies, but here in stone-cold reality, I couldn't get the ignition to work no matter how many times I turned it. As I got out of the car, I caught sight of two wounded soldiers carrying a third, who'd lost half his body in the shelling. They were making for me, hoping I could help them. I felt so terrible that I couldn't assist any of them. I'd been injured by a shell fragment in the bombardment myself and had used up all my bandages stopping the bleeding.

All I could do for these three boys was be there with them, waiting for each of them to breathe their last. After a while, the soldiers urged me to leave them. As a mother, a woman, and an Armenian, that was not an option for me. I stayed there until they passed away.

The one who'd had half his body blown away died first. I was hoping that help would come soon. I did not even ask their names because I was positive we wouldn't be left alone there. When the soldiers breathed their last, I took their bodies inside the cars that I'd been trying to start up earlier. I knew that if I left the corpses outside, the wild boars would get at them. I wanted at least their bodies to stay intact in the cars.

Spring felt terrifying. Outside, birds were flying around, but no one looked up to admire them. There we were, sitting in a café, talking about death, while life was just restarting outside. Maybe in spring, prisoners don't look up at the sky. Maybe Arineh doesn't care anymore how long she has left to live. Maybe life would become more meaningful if we talked about death more. Maybe the birds don't look down on us, either.

I kept searching for a way to find Armenians, but no matter which way I went, I heard Azeri or Turkish soldiers talking to each other. I tried to call one of my friends. My battery was low, and I only managed to make one phone call and ask for some directions to Hadrut. My comrade explained over the phone that they, too, were hemmed in by the enemy. I tried to follow the direction he suggested by phone, but I kept coming up against Azeri soldiers. I tried a different way and eventually reached Mekhakavan.

At first, I had no idea what village it was. I saw a destroyed shop, went in and tried to find a map. On the way to the shop, I met a kitty. I took her along with me, as I knew the dogs might harm her. At least with her, I thought I would feel less afraid, and we could face our enemies together. One of the things I was most scared of was not being killed but being captured. I knew what this enemy was capable of doing to women. I was not scared of being beaten, either, but was petrified that the Azeri soldiers might violate my body. They could rape me, take pictures, and spread them on the internet. I have become more convinced—now more than ever—that they really love defilement.

What a long pause. We stared at each other. Was Arineh insinuating that she did get raped? I couldn't take in what she'd just dropped into the conversation. She lit her fifth or sixth cigarette. She was so smart that she even knew where to take a pause and let me digest the information she had just imparted.

She went on: "I have become more convinced—now more than ever—that they really love defilement." I went to the toilet. I was terrified someone might catch up with me and make me go back and face some more. Running over to the toilet door, I slammed it shut and jammed my whole weight against it. I washed my face, regained some of my strength, and went back to the table.

We entered the shop with the cat. I opened a tin of stew: some for the cat, some for the dogs. Meanwhile, I was scouting around for ways to get out of that place. I stayed there for two days, striking out to the countryside, trying to find any possible exit from the blockade. On October 7th, I was in the village during the day and found there were neither Turkish nor Azeri soldiers there. However, in the evening, they entered the village with tanks. For a moment, I thought they might be Armenians, but fortunately, I caught sight of the Turkish flag in time and the next moment could hear Turkish voices. I ran to the shop again to hide. That whole day, I lay low in the shop. They even entered the shop but did not spot me the first time. The second time, life was not so kind to me.

I don't know how I could have fallen asleep. I guess I was overwhelmed, it was cold, and I had a fever. Anyway, I slept. Maybe if I hadn't, the enemy wouldn't have found me. I opened my eyes from the pain. They were beating me with a huge wooden stick. They wanted to make sure I was dead. After some blows to my head, I told them to stop. I was like a football, being kicked by around 15 men. They tore off my clothes and carried me to a location where they had their new position. On the way, they beat me harshly. Someone pulled my hair, put a knife to my throat, and threatened to kill me. One of the commanders stopped him. After a while, they drove me to their base. I had innumerable bruises on my body. I was completely naked. They gave me an army blanket to wrap myself in. When the enemy soldiers captured me, luckily, I was not wearing an army uniform. That saved my life, as it allowed me to tell them I hadn't been involved in the war and was just a civilian. I managed to mislead them by saying that I was only in that village because the Armenian Government had promised me a house and land there.

Now things were becoming more apparent to me. From what she said, I understood she had not been naked before being captured. It was after the Azeri soldiers found her in the shop and before they took her to their base—where she was given an army blanket to cover herself—that she was naked. She talked of around 15 men beating her and tearing her clothes off in the shop. These are enough indications, then, to suggest that she could have been raped between the shop and the army position.

I was in a room, and the commander asked me whether there was anything I would like to have. I asked for water to drink and to wash my face, as I was caked in blood. And then a journalist came over. I had no idea he was a journalist, as he had an army uniform on. He said he was a commander and told me that I shouldn't worry, there was no danger in store, and that they would just make a short video of me.

They found a blanket, which they put around me. But because I'm fat, it was not big enough to cover my body completely. The journalist gave me an army raincoat, which I had on under the blanket. When they made the video, I intentionally left part of the blanket open, so the Armenians could see the Azeri army raincoat and twig that I was a POW. They hung a grenade from my neck, concealed under the blanket. If I didn't deliver the message I was required to say, they said they'd blow me up. I thought of letting the grenade off because at least that way, as I died, I could take some of them with me. What made me think better of it was the thought that it could have been a training grenade and might actually have no effect at all. That would just prolong the agony. And to be honest, I really wanted to live. Just to live. Not for any particular reason; I simply wanted to be alive.

Not only did I have a grenade hanging from my neck, but there were around 20 soldiers pointing their weapons at me while the video was being recorded. The recording was redone four or five times. I was passing out and had no energy left at all. When beating me up, they also whacked my knees, which made my condition even worse. I was scared and weak. But they made me take medicine, after which I felt awake, fearless, I lost my capacity to think, and everything felt meaningless.

They made the video, then kept me in a car for around half an hour. This half-hour was enough for me to notice what weapons they had imported from Turkey and Israel. I could see how they destroyed the Armenian positions. I could see it was foggy, and they could push a certain button to look through the fog. They could observe the Armenian position unseen and destroy it in a split second. Our soldiers were not prepared for this type of war, and nor was I. We thought it would be like the war in April: a couple of days, and it would all be over.

After they'd shot the video, I was transferred to Baku. They did not blindfold me; they wanted me to see their ammunition. Also, they showed me some big trucks and casually mentioned that they were full of Armenian corpses. It was "a gift for the mothers of Armenia," as one of the Azeri soldiers said. I was powerless to do anything.

I thought about the parents who were still searching for the bodies of their sons. Imagine! Could something like that really happen today? That just felt terrible.

Once we reached Baku, they took me to the hospital. As I entered the hospital, everyone started applauding and saying, "Good job, very nice speech in the video." They left me in the room, then took me to the bathroom and helped me shower while uttering dirty words about me. The doctor had a look at my leg and told the rest of them that I was "not wounded." Ashkhen, that same doctor who had once sworn an oath to help people regardless of their nationality, race, or religion, showed me no help. The same with the nurses; they used so many dirty words when talking to me.

Only the head doctor was a bit different. He spoke to me as a patient, as he realized how scared I was. I was shivering continually. I told him about my diabetes, but he considered it not a serious issue. He did see to it that I got some medicine, though. When the soldiers delivered me to the hospital, my hands were tightly bound, and the blood was barely circulating. I asked the doctor to loosen the bonds, and luckily they decided to untie my hands for the rest of my time in captivity.

In the cell next to mine, there was another wounded Armenian, a soldier whose name was Ashot. The Azeris liked to call all Armenians by the stereotypical Armenian man's name "Khachik," and they even called me Khachik. When this Armenian soldier came round after the operation on his wound, the doctors told him that everything had gone well and he had nothing life-threatening. The nurses came to check on him, and they mockingly asked if his name was Khachik or Khorenchik. And the Armenian soldier answered, "Ashot."

The following day, the nurses issued me some clothes because I was naked and had to meet some representatives of the Human Rights Ombudsman's Office in Baku. There was a woman and a man. The woman was called Nara [a familiar form of Nargiz], but I don't remember the man's name. They brought a dress for me, flip-flops and tights, took me with them, and showed me around Baku. While we had a short walk in the city, they told me about the forthcoming press conference in which I would be required to participate, which could be very important for ensuring my security. People would see me and would think about the need to liberate me.

There we sat in a café in downtown Baku, sipping tea and nibbling baklava, while these human rights people gave me my lines to declaim during the press conference: "Armenia is an aggressive country. The government desires the death of Armenian soldiers." and so on. As the press conference started, I took a step forward and let the journalists fire away with their questions. That way, you see, I only had to answer the questions that the journalists actually asked. There were people from a newspaper, a radio station from Belarus, and Russia. I told them I was a civilian, had never been in the war, and that the Armenians never wanted a war but had to protect their land. And then I added that no one wanted war and that the Armenian mothers were mourning the same way as the Azeri mothers were for their sons.

We took a short breather.

As it dawned on those human rights guys that I was not saying what I was supposed to say, they did all they could to end the press conference. One of the journalists put to me the accusation of the Armenians having recently bombed the city of Ganja, where a child had been killed. I replied, "Are we here to decide who is guilty who is not? You had already been bombarding Vardenis, Goris, the district of Tavush. Those cities are also full of innocent civilians." They'd got my goat now, and I didn't care anymore what might happen to me because I couldn't just let them blame the Armenians for something which is not 100 percent true. Anyway, I was sure they would either not show that press conference at all or cut these bits out.

When they took me back to the hospital, they promised me they'd be back. In fact, though, my darkest days had begun once I returned to the hospital that day. The chief interrogator told me they'd rumbled my lie to them the very day when I'd said I was not a soldier. They'd hacked into my social media accounts right away and found my messages back and forth with my army comrades. Even so, I didn't concede and tried to describe to them other ways one might have participated in the war besides fighting. They were sure I'd been on the battlefield, though, and even that I was a sniper.

It was very violent in the secret service building. They were brutal to our soldiers. The interrogator tried to be civil, offering cigarettes or tea. But as soon as the guards brought me back to my cell, I had the feeling a special squad was stationed there just to rough up the Armenians. They tortured the soldiers ruthlessly; from my cell, I could hear their voices ringing out. In my case, the supervisors came in a couple of times and slapped me about. They wanted me to cry or scream, but I wouldn't react because I did not want to make our soldiers feel even worse. I summoned up all my strength and didn't cry at all.

The truth was I was doing my job: sitting there and let her share her story. She said the war was the worst thing that could have happened to her, whereas back home, we'd been cheering on Facebook as more volunteers joined up for the war. The truth was, it was always those who never experienced war who would wax lyrical about it. The truth was that it was people like Arineh who saw the invalids crawling about, the paralyzed lying helpless, the fields choked with corpses, naked and blackened. After all that, she was still determined to stay strong so that the Azeris didn't see her crying. What pride!

During the interrogation, I often quarreled with the chief interrogator, whose name was Samil Aliyev. Whenever I mentioned the name of the city of Stepanakert, he said it was Khankendi. Whenever I said "Artsakh," he "corrected" me to say "Karabakh." Once, he turned on the radio, and I heard Ara Gevorgyan's rendition of Artsakh. That prompted him to say that we Armenians had "pinched their tunes and musical instruments." I would start arguing with him but couldn't defend my position with vigor. After all, I was, as Samil Aliyev told me, "a guest, and a very unwelcome guest at that." He would also punish me by cutting out the cigarettes. For a smoker, that can be the worst thing. I didn't mind going without food, but I felt very sick without cigarettes. I was on the third floor, in cell number 35. On the same floor, there were Azeri prisoners as well. It was unfair; they would throw our plates on the floor as they brought our meals. And the floor was dirty and dusty.

On October 8th, I was taken from the secret service building and transferred to Baku Prison. Here, it was much better. For the first week, they always gave me enough cigarettes. One of the best things was that they didn't torture our soldiers at that prison. However, the staff over there did make the Armenians shout out dirty words about themselves, like "I am a götveran [a scumbag]," "[Prime Minister] Pashinyan is a götveran," "Karabakh is Azerbaijan," and the like. As soon as one of the guards opened the door, the soldiers had to say these things loud and clear. That's how they humiliated the Armenians.

On November 1st, Arega was put into my cell. "Who could this older woman be?" I wondered. The supervisor explained that she would be my new cellmate. In a way, I was happy, as I would not be alone anymore; at the same time, though, I thought they must have no heart or feelings at all. Arega was 72 years old and had suffered a stroke and a heart attack. They even made both of us call ourselves whores. I begged the guard to let me say it in her stead, as I felt horrible. He made me a deal: I had to get down on my knees and start yelling dirty words. I had to do it. This woman was old enough to be my mother; I just could not let her repeat these disgusting words. Then as I knelt down, the supervisor chortled: "Great job; now Arega doesn't have to stand up or say anything when I enter."

Arega and I stayed together in that cell. We suffered isolation in dark, damp conditions. The bedstead was made of iron and had a wooden board on it. Sure, there was a mattress, but it was so thin, it might have been made of wood as well. The floor was rotten to bits. As I'm overweight, every time I climbed into the bed, it would be pressed deeper into the floor. So I slept on the floor for around ten days. But suddenly it got so cold, there was no heating, we had no warm clothes, and our strength was spent.

When Arega joined me, I took off my warm sweater and trousers and gave them to her. When Arega, her husband, and another older man had been captured, the Azeri soldiers had held them amid mud and cow manure in a farm outbuilding. We had to wash all her clothes. So I gave her whatever I had to wear and made do with some other clothes that the Red Cross had given me during their first visit. There came a time when we were both sleeping on one bed to keep warm. We had a blanket each, but still, it was icy.

We also faced psychological humiliations. Once, I returned from the interrogation room to my cell to find that they'd dumped our whole bread rations for that day in the toilet. The next day, I berated the interrogator that it was not Armenians who'd baked that loaf, and the bread was innocent of any involvement in whatever he was supposed to be investigating me for. Another time, as I was on my way back to the cell from interrogation, I witnessed how they spat on our soldiers' food. They wouldn't let us sleep. For instance, we were made to sit up until 3 a.m. and then were allowed to sleep until 6 a.m. They would storm in, start torturing our men, and look me in the eyes to see if I would cry. I showed no reaction. That was a principle for me, and I did not want to give them the pleasure of letting them see my pain.

There were two shifts in the prison. One of them treated us decently enough. As far as I could make out, they were locals from the city. The guards from the provinces were more violent toward us. They would regularly insult us or ignore a request of ours. But I must also admit, Ashkhen, that job of theirs was a bother. Imagine: one shift had to stay in the prison for a whole week before the next shift would relieve them. They were not well paid, as they told me, but they had to do it. The building was oval-shaped, and it was three-storied: the Azeri male prisoners were on the first floor, the women on the second, and the Armenians on the third floor. We had no chance to stretch our legs. They would give us a bar of soap once a week, with which we both had to take our showers and wash our clothes. Even when we wanted to open the window to let some fresh air come in, they made a big deal of it. We made a point of asking, but it was always in vain. The second shift was not my favorite. They would give us cigarettes if they were in a good mood. The food they brought was pigswill, but we had to eat it. Luckily, when it got colder and colder, they moved us to the second floor. The frost on the third floor was heavy. Later, they turned on the heating.

"One of the most unforgettable days was the taking of Shushi. There was such a huge celebration in the prison. The older woman and I cried. Arega cried because of her daughter, a resident of Shushi; I cried because we had left behind so many corpses of Armenian soldiers in Shushi. The next day, they gave us a special celebratory dish of rice and raisins and some cigarettes. The bread was rotten; we always ate the crust and threw the rest to the birds.

I asked them if there was any chance of us getting back to Armenia. They said only when their compatriots returned to their houses in Karabakh. Although this answer dashed all my hopes, I still dreamt of being home in time for New Year. You can't imagine how happy we were on December 4th when General Muradov appeared in our cell. Arega started crying, knelt down, and implored Muradov to save us. He promised he would get us home before the end of the month. Muradov started asking us some questions, and we tried to answer, but an Azeri soldier piped up and answered on our behalf. The general was apoplectic and yelled at the Azeris, "They have a tongue; they can answer for themselves." I caught a glimpse of the full list of the names of our POWs as Muradov entered our cell. It was a four-page list, and I think there could have been three to 400 captives at two prisons in Baku. In our prison alone, there were around 200 Armenian detainees. The reason they'd transferred us from the secret service building to Baku Prison was only that there were not enough cells at secret service HQ for the new group of Armenian captives.

On December 5th, one of the supervisors entered the room and said that Arega's husband had passed away. I went with Arega to bid her husband farewell. His body smelt utterly foul, and his death must actually have occurred much earlier than December 5th, as he was frozen stiff. He had bruises all over his body and a blue circle on his face where the blood was coagulated. He had been beaten behind his ears as well, and his body was in the condition that you'd expect if they'd crushed him against his bed. He had the pattern of the bedsprings imprinted on his body. One of his arms was severely damaged from overtight handcuffs. I didn't want to go into detail in front of Arega, but what I saw was enough for me to be sure that he hadn't "passed away;" he'd been murdered.

I felt this might be the end of our conversation. A man in a leather jacket with a bouquet in his hands entered the café. More upbeat music came on; the men on the table alongside ours started flirting with one of the waitresses. The whole world was bustling, the café filled up, and I felt that I was a passive entity, absorbed in someone else's story.

> The Red Cross visited me twice. On December 5th, when we found out that Arega's husband had been killed, they came to the prison. I asked the Red Cross, "Weren't you supposed to come on October 23rd?" The Red Cross told me that the Azeri authorities had not allowed them to enter the prison on that occasion and had told them that I had Covid[14] and was "in quarantine." However, the Red Cross did help me write a letter to my friend, in which I told her everything was fine and I that hadn't breathed a word about being in the military. I wanted the Armenians to be sure I hadn't let anything slip about who I was. One of the problems was that I couldn't tell the Red Cross about our true conditions. Although there was no one sitting in on the meeting itself, they were eavesdropping on our conversation from behind the door, and we had to be careful. I wrote on a piece of paper: "Please save us, they're going to kill us," and let the woman from the Red Cross read it.

---

[14] At Baku Prison, owing to the global Covid-19 situation, the Armenian captives were also given medical masks every time they had visitors, or were conveniently "in quarantine," such as in the cases of Arineh or Saro.

During our stay in Baku, there were constant interrogations. They tried putting the frighteners on us:
"If you go to Armenia, people will call you a traitor,
your secret service will not let you breathe freely. Stay
here, or you can go to a third country instead." I said
no: "I can definitely find any solution to my problems
in Armenia, and I want to go home." They even told me
there were 35,000 Armenians living in Baku; everyone
was "happy" and had "comfortable conditions." They
said that President Aliyev "didn't want war" and suggested a humanitarian corridor if we agreed to return
the seven occupied districts [outside Artsakh proper].
This war wouldn't have happened in the first place if
we'd agreed to just that, they said, but the Armenian
Government had wanted their soldiers to be killed. The
Azeris wanted us to hate our government at any price.

Arega got news that she was going to be repatriated on December 9th. The older woman cried and
said she wanted to go home with me. What was very
impressive was that she told me: "Arineh, my daughter, please don't think of harming yourself." I told her
to collect all her stuff and go without saying a word.
She was scared I would commit suicide because I felt
very down and wanted to kill myself in the last few
days. And she knew that now she wouldn't be with
me anymore, I could easily end up doing it: "I don't
have to stay alive because of Arega anymore," were my
thoughts. I knew my death wouldn't change anything:
one prisoner wouldn't make a big difference, but because of General Muradov's visit, I had hopes of being
home by New Year.

When Arega went, I started weakening. On December 11th, I cried for the first time; I'd pent up my
emotions for so long that I just let everything out. Vagif, the supervisor for the day, burst in and asked why

I was crying. I said, "Yes, Vagif agha [Mr. Vagif], I just want to go home." Vagif agha told me to collect my stuff and get ready for my return. I thought he was joking; he assured me he was in earnest. He brought me perfume, trimmed my nails, and helped me get ready. My blood pressure was soaring, and my heart was beating, fit to burst. I was so happy I thought I would have a heart attack then and there.

They brought me some medicine, helped me get my blood pressure down, offered me some cigarettes, and I slowly felt health return to me. I was now with another woman called Gayaneh from the district of Martuni. Gayaneh had been looking after her father in her village, had gone out for water, and the Azeri soldiers had captured her. When we boarded the repatriation flight, I expected it to be full of all of our Armenian captives. My disappointment and grief at seeing it empty made me go crazy again. I started shouting, "I don't want to go home; I will only return when everyone comes with me. Bring all of our soldiers on this flight!" There were only three of us captives on the plane. Muradov told me he would yet bring everyone back and told me to go home. And so we got home [she smiled as she said this].

I asked for the bill, and we left the café. I felt so silly when I found myself wishing Arineh 'all the best' as we said goodbye to each other. All the best with what? She was living in a no-prospects village a long way from the capital. Did I mean all the best with coming to terms with all the unspeakable she'd just had a couple of months ago? Can humans really get used to anything? If so, I wonder how she is feeling now. That day, I returned my tickets for a concert because I wanted to work through her story and could do without the chitchat that would be waiting for me there. A moment earlier, I'd been wanting to get out of the city…

CHAPTER 6

The Horror of Realizing You Are an Animal

I went to Dilijan to get one story but came back with four. I remember interviewing Samvel A. and asking him if he knew any other former captives who would be willing to share their story. Samvel gave me Saro's number. As we struck up a conversation on the phone, I immediately heard he was from my region. We both came from the southern province of Syunik. This put him altogether at his ease, and we firmed up a date for the interview.

My taxi drew up in front of the hotel in Dilijan. As we entered the small hotel room, four other young men were soberly pacing around the room. I started the interview with Saro.

> As the war flared up, our unit was fighting in Jabrayil. We understood we had no chance of advancing; with about a hundred soldiers, we withdrew to Hadrut. On October 15th, the Azeri soldiers blockaded us; only nine of those hundred soldiers survived after intense battles. We stayed blockaded for about five days. We went up and down the hills; no matter which direction we would walk in, we would meet Azeri soldiers. We understood we had no hope of getting out of there. The Armenians could not help us because the surrounding countryside was rife with enemy soldiers. I'd been injured by two shell fragments, both in my waist and in my leg. We all were wounded and had no way of fighting on.
>
> On October 20th, as dawn broke over the battlefield, we were blockaded again. We sat for a moment to catch our breath and then continued walking. Suddenly, we noticed an Azeri soldier. One of my friends ran

after him and shot him dead. At that moment, it felt like it does in the movies: the number of Azeri soldiers suddenly doubling, tripling. Each second, our options for being rescued were becoming more limited. As they increased more and more in number, I understood the Azeris might well capture me. As I'd heard how they would cut off their captives' ears, would torture them to death, it was not an option to let them arrest us. So we fought on.

A breeze was wafting in from a window left ajar. The wisdom of dark days spent in the war was expressing itself through Saro's lips. He wasn't just sharing a story; he was devoted to the conversation. Until he went on with the next installment of his account, he stood there, meditative, hopeless: constantly questioning his existence.

There were 30 of us soldiers in the unit during the war, and as they started bombarding us, we got into the trench. The bombs started falling on us, and I saw many corpses. Bodies torn to pieces. I approached the commander and told him that we had to take the bodies with us. We had to hand them to their mothers. He said, "Young man, in war, you have to be prepared for anything. Here, you witness things that seem to be unreal." These words stuck with me. I thought the mothers of the fallen soldiers would never find their sons' bodies. Every time we joined battle, I would experience some new horror. My comrade was beside me, but within a second, he was killed. Then I would question why he and not I. Of course, I was very grateful to be alive and to have hopes of seeing my parents again, but I wished I had never gone through that hell. I wished I'd been killed on the battlefield rather than being captured by the enemy.

Saro had a problem. He felt ashamed. Even though he'd fought for the motherland, he couldn't come to terms with having been taken captive. The people of Syunik tend to be especially tough, even on themselves.

> We fought for around ten minutes until our ammo was spent. Out of those nine soldiers we'd started the battle with, now only six were still alive—all of them injured. Two of the soldiers were Armenian Special Forces; they'd even been involved in the Four-Day War in April 2016. They started negotiating with the Azeri soldiers and tried to persuade them to stop shooting. They had Turkish flags on their uniforms and were themselves special forces, between 25 and 35 years old. We had one grenade left between us, and we wanted to blow ourselves up. However, one of the Armenian special forces didn't let us, grabbed the grenade, went outside, and threw his hands up. Valer and I were the last out, still thinking of killing ourselves rather than being captured. I told Valer how much I longed to have been one of the killed soldiers; at least they wouldn't feel the pain of becoming a captive. I had only ten bullets; Valer had three.
>
> We had no option but to surrender. They tied our hands, blindfolded us, and took us to their commander. We asked for water. Instead, we received a fist to the face. They took kebab skewers and ran them through our injured bodies. Because, as I mentioned, we had two special forces troops with us, who had different uniforms on, the enemy didn't believe that it was only them who were professionals. I'd only been in the army for two months, but they wouldn't believe I was just a raw recruit. They would torture me, and I would lose consciousness, then they would throw water on my face. As soon as I came to, they would continue

beating me up. I lost consciousness three times. They tortured us non-stop. As I felt what the burden of captivity was, life froze for a moment; I felt no pain anymore. Later, they took us to Hadrut.

In Hadrut, the commander wouldn't let the soldiers continue their violations. He told them that we were injured already, and we would die if we got any more. As soon as the commander left us, though, the soldiers would jump on us and try out their strength. I wanted to be one of the dead soldiers. I understood no Russian, and this was one of the main reasons they humiliated me more. They took our blindfolds off for a couple of minutes, and we worked out we were still in Hadrut.

After they threw us into a beauty salon in Hadrut, we waited a bit until the car came to take us to Baku. When the car arrived, they threw us in the car and started on us with their feet and rifle butts. We were already in the military vehicle when the doctor approached us to look at our wounds. The guys who were still bleeding were taken to the hospital. The doctor didn't take me to the hospital, though, because I'd already been injured for five days, and I wasn't bleeding anymore. The doctor told them I would pull through; they should take me to the hospital if the wound got irritated, he said. They took me to the military police building instead."

In this building, the worst days had begun. I stayed there for four days, and they wouldn't ask me a single question. Had they asked me a question, I would have said I wasn't answering anyway. So they tortured me. They would just come in with police batons and start hitting us. They would torture my mate in his cell, and I would hear his voice from mine. We edged closer and closer to death. Four days later, they took us to the secret service building. After venting their anger, finally, they started the interrogations. They told us that no one would come to rescue us and that after several days of interrogation, they would just kill us. And we thought that if they were determined to kill us anyway, then we wouldn't tell them anything.

No matter what we would or wouldn't share with them, they were going to torture us. In the secret service building, they only used police batons. They showed me some videos of Azeri corpses that Armenians had posted on social media and continued humiliating us. They wanted me to call my military comrades and ask them things about the war. I wouldn't do it. I told them I had no mates left, as they'd all perished on the battlefield. However, once, I offered to make a call because I wanted to let my family know by hook or by crook that I was alive. But the Azeri officers grasped my reason and wouldn't give me a phone.

They well understood that I wasn't giving them any information not because I didn't want to, but because I'd only been in the army for three months when the war started, and I barely knew anything. However, they were convinced I was a special forces guy, and they started using electric shocks to make me talk. First, they threw me on the floor, and when they touched my body with the electrodes, I would immediately lose consciousness. They would then switch off the current, wait until I revived a little, and do it again. Then they would kick me and throw me from one corner of the room to the other until I started bleeding internally.

They transferred me to prison. I was so weak that I couldn't even drink. I was lucky to be with four other Armenian captives who took care of me. I was taken to interrogation a lot because I could speak no Russian, so they thought I had something to hide. Mostly, they wanted to know what we'd done with their dead and anything about Armenia. The interpreter would come for half an hour; after he went, the officers would start with their violations. I'd already been in the cells for 16 days when the Red Cross visited me. They asked me to write a letter to my parents.

I tried, but I couldn't; my hands were swollen from the beatings and the shocks. So a comrade who'd been captured with me helped me write the letter. I had only two sentences in my mind and dictated to my mate: "No matter how many years might pass, I will return." That letter reached my parents within a day. The Red Cross asked me how I was feeling and whether I was being treated decently. I thought they might be playing with us and trying to see whether we would intimate anything to the Red Cross, so I was too scared to say anything. They could see my wounds; they could see I wasn't well, but I told them everything was fine. Then the guards took me back to the cell.

Saro had scars from overtightened handcuffs and restraint cables. He didn't have to shift any clothing to show me; I could see the scarring plainly.

In the secret service building, they again started beating us. Before interrogation got underway, they would beat us, and then once again once we'd finished answering their questions. Even if the interrogator himself didn't torture us, the guards or others in charge would do their dirty work for them. Sometimes, I would be jealous of some of the other captives because the Azeris weren't violent to all of us. To me, they were incredibly full of hatred because they'd found out I was from Syunik. The interpreter had worked out from my dialect that I was from Syunik, and they consider Syunik to be theirs. They truly loathed me.

He was struggling to continue his story. His voice was fighting to hold out. He was unable to accept all the injustice that had befallen him: not only his captivity but the discrimination against him specifically.

> I stayed seven days in the secret service building with another Armenian captive in my cell. His name was Mikael, and he had a severe leg wound. He had a temperature, and the Azeri officers thought he might have Covid. I had to stay with him for 21 days, and the guards told me I now had to be his carer because I'd been the only guy in contact with him for the previous few days. I had to help Mikael go to the toilet and do everything for him because no one would enter the cell for the next 21 days. Mikael was a heavy guy. There were even moments when I missed the Azeri guards entering the cell. I even wouldn't have minded them torturing me, just as long as someone entered the cell. The Red Cross came to visit me during that time, but the Azeri officers wouldn't let them see me or let me read my parents' reply to my letter. They said I had Covid, and no one was allowed to visit me in the cell. The Red Cross gave my parents' letter to the guards to pass on to me, but I didn't receive anything. I didn't even know that my parents had had my letter.

What was the happiest day for you? (I asked this to distract him from the grim atmosphere in the room.)

> The happiest time was the first 17 days when I was with the other four Armenian captives in a single cell. My shoe size was usually 39, but my feet were so swollen that I could barely wear size 45 flip-flops. I couldn't walk. The guys would carry me from the bed to sit on a chair or go to the toilet. I would sit on the chair and

cry because the pain was getting tougher day by day. But when they came and took me off to be tortured, I didn't feel much pain. There came a time when I grew numb to it.

The days rolled by, and we weren't hearing anything about going home. I was terrified. I was afraid I might get used to this situation. Human beings can get used to anything. I felt I was an animal, and I got used to the food, the bouts of torture, the water, and ultimately got used to waking up in prison. The days went by extremely fast, and that scared me more than any torture. I thought I would stay there for years and that waking up there would become routine. If I didn't return by New Year, I was convinced I would spend the rest of my life in that cell.

This was one of my interviewees' sentences that is still embedded in my memory. Saro's face was red, tense, and he hated himself for having become used to a situation that disgusted him more than any other fate.

Yet, he wasn't exaggerating for my sake; his condition was genuinely miserable.

Mikael and I already had a mutual suicide pact. But we also had hope. Mikael had a chance to talk to his family. He would cry because he wanted to call them again. I would cry because at least he'd spoken to them once. We were jealous of each other. He would tell me that at least I'd sent a letter; I would tell him he'd heard his parents' voice. I couldn't understand how out of a small thing, we would start arguing. We would talk about the war; we would think of our killed brothers. I would be hard on myself for being alive while my friends had been killed. I wanted to be among the dead, and I wanted everything to end right there. In the end, we both felt we were losing our minds.

On December 14th, at around 10 a.m., an Azeri guard entered the cell and took me to the interrogation room. They made me write a declaration: "I, Saro M., swear that I am co-operating with the Azeri Government uncoerced in any way." As I was writing, two Azeri soldiers were standing beside me and leveling their guns at me. I had to write it. But I'd also gathered that negotiations were underway, and I was somehow also happy about writing it. Then they told me I had to read the text out loud, and they would make a video of me. I was only too glad to do so because the only thought in my mind was getting back to Armenia. The price of freedom didn't matter by that stage.

Then I got back to the cell and told Mikael what had happened. After a while, he was taken off for interrogation too. But hours passed, and he didn't return. I thought maybe he was refusing to speak, and the Azeri officers were torturing him again. When he returned, he had clenched fists and was very frightened, brooding, and wouldn't say anything. Then he opened his heart and told me that the Azeri officers had given him an e-mail address to contact as soon as he returned to Armenia. If he didn't do it, they threatened, he "could be jailed any time he traveled outside Armenia" because he'd "given his word" by "signing a treaty with the Azeri Government." I tried to calm him down and told him that the main thing was to get home and that they wanted to scare him. We thought of flushing the slip of paper with the e-mail address down the toilet, but then we thought we'd better not: maybe when we got home, they would have ways of checking whether Mikael still had it.

Then they opened the door, and we had to go with them. I carried Mikael, as he couldn't walk. We sat in the car. Till the last moment, they punched us in the face. We reached the airport, heard some helicopter noise. But we thought we were going to be taken to Armenia by car, and it was very agonizing, as we had to kneel down on the car seat. Mikael had leg wounds, his left leg was completely out of action, and both my legs were excessively swollen.

I told Mikael we had to survive; we'd been through so much that getting through the last act was imperative for both of us. We arrived at the airport. They opened the car door, and we saw the Russian general, Muradov. We reached the plane, and there we met my comrades, and for the first time, I felt happy again. The nightmare was behind us. When we landed in Armenia, people gave us a heroes' welcome. I hadn't known there were so many soldiers in captivity; I thought those of us on the flight were the only ones.

During the war, it was not so much that staying alive was precious to me, but it was the grief that my family would go through if I died that made me struggle on. I wanted to live to save my parents from mourning. They had no news of me; they even went to the morgues to see if they could identify anyone who'd been serving with me. My uncle went missing in action in the 1990s, and my grandma always waited for his return. Back then, the Red Cross told my family that my uncle's group had been captured. Now, years later, history was repeating itself in our family. My father knew how it felt to be in a war. As he'd never heard from his brother again, he was sure that this time, I must be either killed or captured. He made funeral preparations and was getting ready to carry on the search for me among the corpses of Armenian soldiers. After two weeks, he heard that our group had been wiped out by bombing and that they would bring our corpses home soon.

When I returned, I felt I was also bringing my uncle back with me.

I talked to Saro again after he was returned to the ranks of the army. I had concerns for his welfare, evidently more than the government did. He was only 18 years old when the war broke out. He fought, he was captured, heavily traumatized. But, goodness, how did he manage to recover and go back to serving again?

CHAPTER 7

Injustice: The Bitch the World Can't Shake Off

Karen (a man's name in Armenia) and Saro were from the same military unit and had served in Jabrayil. He was also in the diminutive hotel room in Dilijan with me. Karen was very laid-back and constantly interrupted the interviews with some interjection about his luck at being treated surprisingly well by the Azeri soldiers.

> As the war escalated, we got orders to go to the front. We put up resistance for a couple of days, and then we had to withdraw to Hadrut. Already on October 9th, most of Hadrut was taken by Azeri troops. In Hadrut, we had gone through intense fights and bombardments. At some point, we worked out we were under blockade, and we had to back up to think of a solution. Both my legs were injured by rifle rounds. Our squad was exceptional: one of the soldiers, Arayik, was a ranger, I was a specialist on the PK machine gun, Erik was a crack sniper, Rob was an anti-tank missile targeteer, and Narek [not the same Narek as was in the hotel room with us] was a grenadier.
>
> We stayed under blockade for 43 days. One day, Arayik here [who was also in the hotel room in Dilijan but declined to be interviewed] went out to reconnoiter. On his return, he brought soldiers' boots with him from someone's house in Hadrut. We told him they weren't Armenian military boots because when we had a look at them, we found a Turkish flag printed on them. So we told him to take them back pronto and leave them right where they'd been. So Arayik

took them back again, and this time he brought some persimmons, pomegranates, and other food back with him. It was because of him that we managed to survive for that long. We were in the village of Vank, in Hadrut district, and radioed ahead that we were "holed up at Vank in Hadrut." Well, the balls-up in rescuing us was that because the noun vank means "monastery" in Armenian, our officials thought we were hiding "at a monastery in Hadrut City." But no, we were in a village called Vank.

As early as November 21st, we were out of water. When the Azeris completely overran Hadrut, they cut off all the utilities for a while. So we would make an omelet with candle heat or swigged cold fruit compotes from the cellar of the house we were hiding in. Soon, everything had run out. But picture this: just as we were about to go thirsty, a bomb fell on a bowser truck parked in front of the house. Out of curiosity, we went outside to have a peep. We saw water had started leaking from the blown-up tank. It was a miracle.

The city of Hadrut lies in the middle of a gorge, and we were on the crest of an overlooking hill. As the Azeri soldiers took control of the city, they started sweeping from bottom to top, and we were moving locations, if possible, the other way: downhill. When we managed to relocate to a new house, we would check the cellar first. If we found no stored food in a house, we knew they'd beaten us to it. The enemy soldiers had also ransacked the place where we stayed the longest. There was not a single shelf left intact; only the cellar was still closed. We assumed they'd given the door a shove, and as it hadn't opened, they'd just moved on.

We stayed in that cellar for 40 days: from October 9th until November 21st. Then, starting from November 21st, we moved from the cellar to the rooftop. We were actually still down in the cellar when they ransacked the house, but because of the darkness, when they opened the cellar door, they couldn't see us. It was after they left that we changed place, as we were sure they'd be back. We were up on the roof as we watched them driving the animals away from the house. We stayed up there, but we knew they'd find us eventually. That same day, November 21st, one of the Azeri soldiers climbed up the roof. He was scared witless to see five guys sitting there. It was very unexpected for him. He'd left his rifle downstairs, but we were tooled up.

We didn't open fire, though, because we were well aware a whole company would be after us if we did. So resistance was pointless: we had not enough bullets and very little strength, as we were rationing ourselves to five spoonfuls of food a day. We were hoping the Armenians would come and get us out of there, and we had no idea Hadrut was not in our hands anymore. The Azeri soldier yelled, grabbed a stick on the double, and pointed it at us. We stood up and walked down the stairs. There, we met many more soldiers, and we had to explain to them what we'd been doing on the roof. We told them the whole story.

The Azeris promised to help us. They said they would take us to Baku and that within ten days, we'd be back in Armenia. So we thought that would be a better option than staying in that house and waiting for the Armenians to show up.

Might have taken them 30 years, eh.

So young, but a killer wit.

They told us to show them where we'd stashed our weapons. We refused at first. They blindfolded me, made me kneel down, pointed a gun at my head, and told the rest of them to dig a grave for me. They wanted to shoot me and bury me right there. We put our heads together and agreed that since the territory was theirs to comb over anyway, they'd find the cache sooner or later, whether I copped it or not. So we showed them our artillery store, where they made a video of us, and then they took us to their military base in Hadrut.

The interrogation started with Arayik. One of the Azeri commanders asked him if he could speak Russian. He answered no, and the commander punched him in the face and quipped, 'If you don't know Russian, how come you just said nyet?' That got a hearty laugh out of us, and the enemy was crestfallen to see that we had such spirits, even in captivity. One of them took a knife and slashed my head open. They also used different objects to torture us. After a while, I was so numb that they would punch me, and I would feel no pain anymore. Also, the mere fact that I wasn't alone made me stronger. After hours of beatings, we were taken to Baku. First, we were taken to the hospital, where a nurse took a cursory look at my wound. I told her that the Azeri soldiers had made the cut, and, while muttering, "Should have taken it right off," she emptied a whole bottle of zelenka antiseptic on my head and let me go. The green stuff burned my head; for days, I couldn't use a pillow.

After this ordeal, we were taken to a military base in Baku. They started the process of interrogation. Every piece of information was exacted at a price: a hefty blow. Then they took us to the secret service building. I started talking to the guards, asking them questions like what a particular word would be in Azeri. At that building, I was treated well. Although some of them would curse us, most of them were nice enough to me. In my cell, I was utterly alone, and it was unrelieved tedium. Only for the last 20 days did my mate join me in the cell. From that day on, I didn't even notice the days passing by.

I started acting as if I was going gaga. I would pipe up with ballads at the top of my lungs about the bold Armenian soldiers. They would open the cell door and ask me what the hell I was bawling. I would tell them about my motherland, as I missed it so much. I did it all on purpose, so they'd get tired of me and send me packing. I wanted them to become sick of me. They would give me cigarettes or sweets, just so I'd shut my mouth. Or sometimes they would even beat me up, but that wouldn't help.

Karen was chattering away as if he'd not been in enemy hands. He was so full of how well he got on with the guards and how well he got them to treat him. But Saro was sitting right beside him and was repeating over and over again: "I couldn't understand the hatred they bore me. Where's the bloody logic? I was the same age as Karen, we served in the same unit, but unlike him, I experienced an extreme level of humiliation."

There were also some positive memories. On New Year's, they gave me a Santa Claus as a gift [a not unusual time to give Christmas gifts in former Soviet countries], and also pen and paper. One day, the guard opened the door, looked at me, and asked if I had any requests. I asked if I could call my family. He told me to wait a minute. Around 11, he opened the door together with someone else, pointed his finger at me, and left again. In the evening, he returned and told me that he had "bad news:" "I am taking you to a hellhole; you will be tortured to death there." But actually, we went off to pick up Garik [whose story is also included in this book] and then headed to the airport. For a moment, I thought maybe they were taking us to Turkey for special treatment, but when I asked the Russians on the plane, they told me we were about to land in Armenia, at Erebuni airport.

Saro added: "Even if they didn't use torture, the psychological stress was enough." Then Narek said that just hearing the Azeri language being spoken the whole time was enough for him to feel he was going mad. Karen, on the other hand, was much more upbeat. He said he was treated well. He had only been in the army for three months, and the Azeris realized he was too young to have committed any transgressions; at least, this was what he reckoned they must have believed. No such luck for Saro.

CHAPTER 8

The Bitter Price of Freedom

Narek (N.) had arrived in Dilijan just a day before I called on him. We sat talking about the brutality of human nature and the possible causes of the Azeris' obscene hatred of Armenians. Narek still had black bags under his eyes; he was one of the most softly-spoken of all my interviewees, making me concentrate extra hard not to misunderstand anything. The silence was broken by the solemn commencement of his story.

> From the start of the war, I was fighting in Talish and then in Mataghis. Already on October 2nd, we lost Mataghis and had to withdraw in the direction of Martakert. During our withdrawal, I realized we'd left a wounded man behind. I helped him to the vehicle, and when I looked around again, there was literally no one in sight. I had no chance of catching up with my platoon again, so I started walking in the direction of Martakert on my own. On the way, I met other soldiers, and we formed a gaggle. By this time, we were retreating from Talish to Mataghis. When we reached the Fourth Battalion dugout, we took a ten-minute break.
>
> I really don't know what exactly happened, but there came a moment when some of the soldiers went out to tend to the wounded and get them to the hospital. After a couple of minutes, I went outside to join them and realized everyone had cleared off. There were only seven of us soldiers left: to be precise, six volunteers and I. None of us knew the terrain or the way out. We struck out, hoping to find a road to reach the others, but it was in vain.

Narek was only 18 years old. He had been in the army only for one month and 15 days when the war started. So had the others in that small room.

> We knew approximately where we were, but it was impossible to move around. The Azeris were bombarding us heavily, and we also had some wounded. We took shelter in the Fourth Battalion's bunker for the night. But at dawn, it became apparent that if we ventured out, the enemy would make mincemeat of us in a matter of seconds. Shells were falling every other moment. We got some food and water together, as we were hoping to walk out of there no matter what happened.
>
> As the moment of truth approached for us to make a dash for it, we heard voices. We couldn't make out whether they were speaking Armenian or Azeri. But we were basically sure anyway that they must be Armenians, as Mataghis was a very strategic area, and there was no way the Azeris could have occupied it, or so we thought. We thought we could make out their voices speaking Armenian." (In another interview, Haik, who was with Narek in the same bunker, said that the language sounded like the dialect of Armenian spoken in Artsakh—which has a Turkish lilt to it—and so they'd taken them to be their own troops).[15] "Hayk and Razmik went out and asked if they were Armenians. The Azeri soldiers did a double-take, and Razmik told them not to run away, saying that we all were Armenians and that there was nothing for them to worry about. They started taking potshots at us, and

---

[15] Crossing the Border: Haik shares his story. Online interview in Armenian: https://www.youtube.com/watch?v=aaw9ornhYvs

Haik immediately closed the bunker hatch and leaped off the steps. We managed to throw ourselves back in the bunker, after which a grenade followed.

Fortunately, the bunker was L-shaped, so when they threw the grenade in, the blast didn't reach us: it exploded in the entrance, and we were at the back around the corner. When they chucked it, we shut up, so they would think they'd got us. They scrammed without coming down to check. We knew, though, that the area was occupied, and we were blockaded. We also knew that the Fourth Battalion had an armory. Hearing footsteps again, we thought they'd stumbled across the armory and would just come in all guns blazing and finish us all off. But no, they just took whatever they wanted and left again. Maybe they really did think we were dead. At any rate, they forayed into the bunker every day. We were in the bunker; they were on top of us. They would even kip there. We would wait until they nodded off before having a bite to eat. We stayed there for around 20 days: food was one thing not in short supply, as that bunker was a field store for the Armenian troops. We had our fill.

On October 22nd, fresh Azeri troops relieved the others. This lot was more gung-ho and had orders to get us. This time, they barged the door and made as if to come down. Hayk yelled up to them, telling them not even to think about it, or we'd let them have it. We did this on purpose, so they would get it through their heads we were armed to the teeth. In reality, it was obvious to us that while we had limited ammo, theirs was inexhaustible. We started shooting, and they let rip. We had no bullets left and only three grenades. We pulled the pin of one of them and threw it at them, but it glanced off the hatch and flew back in our direction. Some of our mates were hurt. These new Azeris also knew the build of the bunker and realized we were a long way back, out of harm's way. So when they forced the door, they flung their grenade with all their might to reach us at the back. We still had two grenades in reserve for the worst case.

Time to negotiate, then. They were trying to explain the possibility of repatriating us through the Red Cross. But to us, it was shameful to throw our hands up and stop fighting. Then Hayk told them, "You and we both are both some mother's son: please, at least promise to return our corpses to our mothers after we top ourselves." The Azeris replied, "Die if you must, but sod off back to your own country first and peg it there."

I wasn't expecting, in the least, what Narek told me next.

So some of the guys went out first. The rest of us stayed behind. No one doubted our patriotism, but either way, the end was death. So even if they lopped off my ear or leg, at least I might be able to get back to my parents, at any price, and see my mum again.

This is the retort to anyone who writes a smug Facebook screed laying into the men who surrendered. Guess what? Life is a precious gift; try finding anyone who's prepared to give it up.

Besides, I was terrified. I decided to give myself up, but we still had those two grenades. Should the Azeris turn violent, we could blow ourselves up and take them with us. We were lucky, though. These were Azeris with a heart, and they were very respectful toward us. They helped the wounded and offered us a smoke. In return, we gave them Garni, an Armenian cigarette, as we had some with us. Everything was fine until they took us to the border. We stayed there around an hour.

A general dropped by and told us we had no cause for alarm. He was dropping hints that they had two "big fish" held in Armenia and would exchange them for us small fries. He said he was going to make sure we were looked after, and no one would do us any harm. But even as he was leaving, the soldiers started beating us up. We called to the general to get a grip on his men. He trained a searchlight on us, so he could see if case anyone had a go at us. We were shocked at how well we were treated. The general told us how different the Azeris were from Armenians, in the sense of them being "much nicer people" than us. The soft approach was something we weren't prepared for, as we knew how savage the enemy could be.

They told stories of what cruelties Armenians had committed back in the day. It was wartime, and in war, everyone does things they would never think themselves capable of on civvy street. No matter whether Armenian or Turk, people can become so brutal. Anyway, this was a surprising turn of events for us, as we knew how ruthless they could be, but also how kind they presented themselves to the world as being. We thought, "If only we'd known you sods were going to be so nice to us, we wouldn't have stayed down in that blasted bunker for three weeks."

A part of me refused to accept this. At the very least, it seems naïve for senior Azeri officers to impress upon Armenian soldiers "how cruel their people could be" while at the same time failing to acknowledge how many massacres their own people have perpetrated against the Armenians and how many of those still go unrecognized. That part of me reacts dismissively whenever I hear such statements: cut the crap, please. Armenians who let these narcissists make them cringe for "Armenians having done cruel things to them" really need to read some history.

Armenians who feel guilty about Khojaly should put the events in their context and consider the contemporary pogroms in Sumgait, Baku, or Maragha. While atrocities—including any events that happened in Khojaly—cannot and should not be justified, it is strange to expect the Armenians to just bow their heads and let their erstwhile next-door neighbors banish or kill them and remain sheepish. So if we're talking cruelty, let's start with Azerbaijan's cruelties.

We sat in the car, and again, there was no violence or brutality. The guys asked for cigarettes, and they even obliged. Ruben took out a pack of Garni and lit up. Even then, they didn't do anything. We were baffled. I thought of the sheer oddness of being in captivity yet not experiencing the cruelty we used to hearing about in the past. I was sure there was something wrong and reckoned the whole situation was about to change.

We arrived and were taken to their military police base. As soon as we got there, the violence started. I told the guys, "Now we've arrived" [with a chuckle]. We were handcuffed. They would beat us and interrogate us simultaneously. They wanted every last scrap of information, starting with the names of our commanding officers, right through to the moment they'd lifted us. I told them I'd served only a month and couldn't remember many of their names. They wouldn't believe me and reached for the electric shocker. I still didn't tell them any names. After some fun with my body, they just left me. We stayed with the military police for five days, and every single day we were tortured brutally. On October 29th, they took us to Gulistan Prison, and from that day on, they didn't touch us anymore.

Oh? Perhaps they were nicer sorts over there and had never heard of electric shocks?

I was in a cell with my mate Armen. The cell was clean, and they would also come round every other day and get us to clean it. I stayed in captivity for 53 days. I got home on December 14th. While in captivity, I didn't speak much. Armen was a right chatterbox; I wasn't nearly as talkative. In the end, we'd run out of topics to discuss anyway. On November 13th, the Red Cross visited me, giving me more hope. At least they knew I'd been captured. Seizing the moment, I told them that some doctors should look in on us because Armen had been injured. They asked for his name and registered him as a POW as well. It was during that visit that they told me that the Azeri soldiers had taken Shushi. It was the worst day of my life. I knew we were going to lose the war. We also wanted it to be over as soon as possible because the sooner it ended, the more lives would be spared."

As the Red Cross guys were about to leave, they asked me if I needed anything that they could bring me during their next visit. This made me very downcast, as it dashed my hopes again of an early release. There was no hint of me returning any time soon, it seemed. On December 2nd, the Russian general, Muradov, entered our cell and told us that we would be exchanged for the two terrorists being held in Armenia—so these were the "big fish" hinted at earlier. The Red Cross paid us another visit on December 12th and asked me if I wanted to write a letter to my family. I answered no; as far as I was concerned, it was better for them to hear I was dead than captured. I was ashamed. However, the Red Cross insisted on how important it was for the family to receive a letter from me, and I relented. I arrived home faster than the letter. I felt horrible, as I knew the price the Armenians had had to pay to free us. Those two terrorists deserved to rot in jail. Be that as it may, we called on the Tsakanian family once home and thanked them from the bottom of our hearts for saving our lives. It was thanks to their generous and agonizing decision that I got to return to Armenia.

Narek was among the 44 captives who returned home on December 14, 2020. The toll exacted was the return of two Azeri saboteurs, Hasan Hasanov and Shahbaz Guliyev (their accomplice Dilgam Asgarov was shot while resisting arrest), who had killed the 17-year-old Smbat Tsakanian. They were both taken alive and sentenced to imprisonment in Armenia: life for Askerov and 22 years for Guliyev. The family agreed to free them in exchange for returning all the Armenian POWs held in Baku. However, one can't rely on the other side in life, especially when the other side is Azerbaijan (or Aliyev dictating what Azerbaijan does).

CHAPTER 9

The Worst Scars Will Stay in the Mind

His voice was quaking, and he was nervously cracking his fingers, which could be interpreted as being haunted by his dark memories.

I had to do something. As I was the only person in the hotel room who was in a position to alleviate the situation, I broke the silence by pointing at the door and asking him to open it. The air in here was slowly choking me.

Uncertain of what to do, I invited him to venture out onto the balcony. He was a small man of sturdy gait. He opened the door, and then I cautiously added: "You know, Samvel [H.], next time I'm in Dilijan, I just have to go camping in this forest; it's pure magic." After coaxing a smile out of him and listening to him open up about his passion for camping, I knew I had won his trust. I headed back into the room again and launched my first question.

In what area were you fighting during the war, Samvel?

> I was serving in the Armenian army. As the war escalated, we were taken to Artsakh without even knowing where exactly. I thought we must be at a dedicated military base, which would most likely be one near the border. Then, in case reinforcements were needed during the war, we could join the rest of the soldiers.

"Were you not in Qubadli?" Narek asked suspiciously. (Narek (N.) was one of the former captives who was in the room with us.)

"They said it was Qubadli, but he can't be sure, as he had never been in those parts before," Saro hastily intervened, seeking to address the skepticism on Narek's behalf.

"I just can't be sure where I was," Samvel said, clearing his throat. His cold eyes pierced me as though he was trying to satisfy himself that at least I wasn't judging him. I did my best to stay out of this grudge, carefully hiding my perplexity behind a mask of polite neutrality. "We were in arduous fights. In the thick of the battle, I could hardly see any Armenians. Only four of us were still on the battlefield, completely cut off from the rest of the soldiers. We realized they had retreated."

"Let me take you through how the command of a retreat on the battlefield works," Saro intervened again, being careful to make sure I kept up with the military terminology. "When troops decide to fall back, a designated group of soldiers, called the covering fire group, advances and opens fire until all the rest have managed to withdraw. And then the withdrawn forces start rearward fire until the covering fire group has also made it to a place of safety. Well, in this case, the guys who had withdrawn did not wait for Samvel and his comrades to make it out from providing the covering fire for them. They just left them behind on the battlefield."

Samvel corroborated Saro's explanation and continued the story.

> To this day, I don't know if they chickened out or just hadn't noticed that the four of us had been left behind. Anyway, it was just me, the captain, and two other privates now. It was also completely dark, and we'd lost our bearing. We followed the captain, thinking that at least he ought to know the way. Crossing so many ditches, losing all sense of direction, we just dived into enemy territory. On the way, one of us disappeared, for reasons unclear. We couldn't understand how he was suddenly just not beside us anymore.

Do you at least remember what day it was?

This may sound absurd, but I didn't know what day

it was. We had walked the entire night. With the first rays of dawn, another firefight flared up at once. One of our mates fell in battle, and the captain was injured. I was still unscathed. The captain and I managed to escape. With a supreme effort, I managed to haul him off the battlefield to some cover. Finding a shelter behind a massive hillside rock, we caught our breath for a couple of minutes. His wounds were quite severe, and he'd lost a lot of blood. I took his clothes off and applied a tourniquet his leg to staunch the bleeding. I thought of scouting for help and told the gaffer I was going off for assistance. And then...

We fell silent for a while. The dénouement of this account was hard on all of us, especially on Samvel. Clutching his head between his hands and collecting his resolve to share more, he still had me riveted at the juncture where he'd been left alone with his captain. By this point, I had a feeling that I knew him. Samvel looked at me, and I returned his gaze, as I wanted him to continue, but I felt terrible pushing him even non-verbally to reopen his wounds.

After slogging on for what felt like a lifetime, I could see the silhouette of a village in the distance. It was not exactly clear, but it wasn't completely obscure either. From far away, the sun's rays were reflecting off it and dazzling me. After a while, I found myself in the village I'd spotted from afar. I entered one empty house after the other. I was opening the doors and screaming, "ANYONE, PLEASE, I NEED HELP." My efforts were futile. And then I gave up hope of finding anyone. I was so exhausted by this point that I had not realized I was already in Azeri-held territory. It was not our territory there anymore. Their artillery was shooting from about 300 meters away from me, and I thought those were our soldiers.

I had to cross a blown-up bridge. I was walking over it, just like any human would walk on a normal day. I had my rifle on my shoulder, not knowing what was about to come.

It took me a while to understand the nuance of his sentence. "Walking just like humans would walk" was a unique occurrence in wartime. On the battlefield, soldiers like Samvel had to become accustomed to running, bending down, and scuttling away on all fours for an extended period of time. At that moment of crossing the bridge, Samvel had realized he was too relaxed, as if it was just a Sunday morning stroll and there was no threat to his life.

I had drifted dangerously from reality, as I was too absorbed in my thoughts by this point. I reached the broken section of the bridge while still mentally turning over possible ways of saving the captain's life. At that moment, I heard whispers around me. The idea of turning around felt like walking into a death trap. But I realized I had no choice. At the other end of the bridge, I noticed around seven soldiers wearing Armenian army uniforms. I ran toward them, shouting, "Guys, what a Godsend, you came to save me! Hurry, guys, we need to help the captain."

Samvel involuntarily touched his face as though his cheeks were burning. He mumbled miserably: "I thought they were Armenians."

They started speaking Azeri, and the bullets started whizzing past my ears. I managed to throw myself behind a wall beside the bridge. I started feeling over my body, checking I wasn't bleeding; my legs were still there, and I was lucky enough to be alive. I took my gun off my shoulder. I remembered I also had a grenade, which I thought I had lost. I was terrified, as I felt as though I'd lost my ability to breathe, and my heart was straining from beating so fast. As I took my gun, I felt something heavy like metal scratching my neck. It was the grenade.

I was sure I was going to die anyway, so it was only fair to fight to the death. I immediately pulled the grenade pin and threw it in the enemy's direction. The explosion of the grenade burst the silence. The shooting started up again. It was time to attempt a getaway. The dense smoke was also oppressing me, attacking my throat, making it difficult to breathe. I was emptying my rifle as if I wanted to expend every bullet in the magazine and hurry up and die. I could barely see a thing. The smoke and dust were a curtain between the two parties, both wanting to kill the other to stay alive. I knew I only had 16 rounds, but the shooting felt endless.

I slumped back in my chair; I was too sore and tense to continue. It was the fourth interview I'd conducted that day: Saro, Narek, Karen, and then Samvel. I took off my earrings, as even they were now weighing me down. Only Samvel's voice was invading my ears and breaking my heart. There were six of us in a poky hotel room with the windows and doors shut.

Though we knew we had to take another break, I couldn't help but wonder how his story ended. I soon found out.

I felt a sniper following me. In my mind, I kept picturing different ways of reaching Armenian lines. I thought of jumping over the bridge, then realized I wouldn't make it over. A little below the bridge, there was an iron fence. I jumped onto that and tumbled directly into the river. It was very rocky and muddy. Falling on the stones, I hurt my leg. I gathered my strength and tried to cross the river. At some point, I stumbled on a rock and couldn't keep my balance anymore.

The river carried me along for about 20 to 30 meters. Then I grasped a tree branch and got myself out. After this long adventure, I manage to throw the deadweight of my body under a tree. Once I'd recovered enough to realize I should move to a better position, I observed my surroundings first. It was as if a voice was telling me to have a good look around before making any steps. You can't imagine, Ashkhen: it was a minefield. My heart pounded, and I started sweating and shivering. Sometimes, I don't even know where all the strength came from that possessed me at that moment. With each step, I was passing through that minefield. I was only too aware that I was dicing with death. I reached a hillock, lay down, and started kenning the surroundings again. Isn't that something? I had a rifle, but no ammo, no grenade, no knife, nothing to protect or even to harm myself.

While observing and churning over every possible outcome, I sensed other human beings next to me. Azeri soldiers were blocking me in. This time, death was inevitable, I thought. I was hoping a bullet would kill me because if it didn't, those guys would, with their bare hands.

No, no, it was impossible. Although I already knew Samvel ended up captured that day, I was getting too emotionally involved in his story and could not accept the reality. Enough! My heart was about to fail me. I closed my eyes and counted to ten to cool myself down and bring myself back to documenting role. Samvel had mentally left us and was all alone in the room. He looked altogether willing to tell more, but he was unhappy and hurt, scared and helpless. I hated the oppressive silence of that room.

They told me to put my hands up and not make any sudden movements. They removed my clothes and tore my cross off. I could see Azeri, Turkish and Pakistani flags on the soldiers' uniforms. They were armed to the teeth. Their weapons were very modern, with night sights on them. I started thinking of my rifle, which didn't even shoot straight. It would just jam from time to time. No doubt it needed cleaning out. That would take extra time—something we don't have in wartime. After opening my military ID booklet, they tossed away the image of a saint I had stored between the pages, blindfolded me, and trussed up my hands and legs.

He took a deep breath and continued.

They took me to a cattle shed, where I was kept for a while. Then, a while later, they took me outside, threw me on the ground, and removed my blindfold. When my eyes had grown used to the light, I lost count of how many Azeri soldiers there were on the scene. As I lay there at their feet, more and more men started showing up. As one of the generals arrived, he opened his mouth to execrate the Armenians. Having gone through so much, I couldn't tolerate this behavior and started using the same filthy language back at them. In captivity, doing something like that means slowly but surely giving them more of a reason to kill you.

They started beating me with a metal rod. I wanted them to wallop me so that I could finally die. Then they made me say, "Karabakh is Azerbaijan," "Pashinyan is a götveren." As I refused, the soldiers continued to pummel me. I was being beaten up with rifle butts, with wooden sticks, with hands and feet. They even made me sit under a pomegranate tree and started pelting me with pomegranates. I crouched down on the ground, hoping to draw my last breath and get it over and done with.

That satisfied their thirst for beating one more Armenian, so they left me under the tree for a while. After what seemed like an eternity, a pick-up car arrived and took me to another type of hell. I wasn't even quite out of the car yet when I felt continuous strokes of fists greeting my chin. By the time I arrived in Baku, I couldn't move a single muscle in my face.

You didn't have to be particularly sensitive or compassionate to empathize with Samvel's story. Samvel was an interesting guy, as well as being really stylish, neat, and modest. However, my guess is that nobody will ever know what horrendous effects this war has caused these young men.

I was already being held at a military base in Baku by now. Here, they resumed the torture. I was thrown into the open courtyard of the secret service building. This time around, they didn't care who might see them laying into me. In this arena, there were two of us: an older man and me. His name was Albig. After making it through another round of torture, we were taken inside the prison. On the way, an Azeri soldier hit me from behind; I hit the asphalt full-on with my face. Handcuffed and blindfolded, I'd lost my balance.

Don't ask me how I made it to the second floor of the prison. While I was in the cell, Azeri servicemen would pass by, enter and kick me. Their hatred of Armenians was limitless, it seemed. After keeping me in the cell overnight, the Azeris took me to a pitch-dark basement the next day. There, I could hear the screams of the same old man as before. They were literally beating him to death. After a while, I implored them, "Please don't beat him anymore. He's on the verge of death. Beat me instead." The old man did not even have a T-shirt on, and it was freezing down there. As you'd expect, my request fell on deaf ears. I don't know if he was still breathing at the end of it. They commanded me, "Take this corpse and throw it in the boot of the car." I started crying. I said, "I can't do it. I won't do it." Ashkhen, I wanted to die—and, deep down, I was so jealous of the old man. The tortures were getting more severe each day.

On the third day, I was taken to a secret service bureau, where they wanted information about anything I knew. Even when they grasped that I had just started my military service and didn't possess any secret information, the humiliation didn't stop. On the grounds of the secret service building, they used police batons to continue the physical violence. Once, we were in the lift, and they beat me up so hard that I went temporarily deaf. These interrogations were never-ending. They asked me the next question without even waiting for the previous answer, and the interrogations were usually accompanied by beatings. One day, they applied electric shocks to my chest and back. They didn't do that for a protracted period of time, though. I think they just wanted to scare me. I was terrified whenever they were beating other Armenians.

Typically, during these interrogations, I could hear the voices of other Armenians from the room next to mine. I felt utterly miserable when some of the guards came and removed the electric shocker, the police baton, the rope, and the whip from the room I was in. After a couple of minutes, I felt as though I had lost the ability to talk. I was so frightened when other Armenians were screaming and crying. It was excruciating to hear.

I set up my bed as a shield between my torturers and me; as soon as they entered, I would run and squat under it. But, to be sure, that didn't stop them from taking me out and continuing with their mission. At one point, they ordered me to sing a song, so I did. A song about Armenian tank drivers, Tankistner, was what I gave them.[16]

But Samvel, was there any specific reason they were so cruel to you?

You know, Ashkhen, I think if I had done the things they had wanted me to do from the outset, they wouldn't have been as brutal. I just thought I was going to die anyway. I held out no hopes of returning to Armenia, so I wanted to give them every reason to kill me the sooner. At some point, though, I understood they were not going to kill me, and that's when I started obeying their commands. I started saying on demand, "Karabakh is Azerbaijan." Once, they even asked me if I believed in what I said.

Samvel's facial expression bore a message. Would someone who was in a war, facing death, in the land called Artsakh, and who had lost his friends there, believe it to be part of Azerbaijan?

After some horrifying days in the secret service building, the Azeri servicemen took me to the prison in Baku. I shared a cell with Tigran, Ruslan, Samvel [A.],

---

[16] The song is available on YouTube at: https://www.youtube.com/watch?v=KIv30Jg43aE

Vahé [whose story ends this book], and Saro. All of them have since made it home.

At the start, I couldn't eat anything; the very idea of touching food was disgusting to me. Tigran kept telling Saro and me to eat something. After a couple of days, it all felt normal. We were famished. We didn't care what lay ahead of us. At one point, I caught myself feeling positively happy that I wasn't alone anymore. The days in the secret service building were the worst time. Not only was the torture unbearable, the loneliness was also very depressing. At Baku Prison, it wasn't so hard: we could talk and support one another and share our dreams of returning home.

Did you also have a visit from the Red Cross?

The guard came into our cell and called my name. He told me to put my Covid mask on and come out. Usually, when I had to leave the cell, I had to go out to the corridor, turn to face the wall, and wait for them to take me off somewhere. This time, I went through the usual motions, but they pointed me to walk to a room by myself and told me a girl was waiting for me. I didn't know that she was from the Red Cross. She asked me, "Do you speak Russian?" I answered, "A bit." When I saw the emblem of the Red Cross on her badge, I felt safe. She set up a phone call to my parents. I don't know what compelled me to tell my family I would be home by December 15th. I just wanted to give them hope, and that was the best I could do at that moment. Ashkhen, imagine the coincidence: the plane took me home on the morning of December 14th! The day I landed in Armenia was the happiest day of my life. And the saddest day was when we were treated to a special victory dish in the cell for the fall of Shushi.

When Azerbaijan took Shushi,[17] there was a massive jolly in Baku Prison.

Samvel's story was etched in my memory in a way no other was. I felt so connected to him and his story that it was after interviewing him that I decided to start writing my book. One thing that consoled me was that Samvel was still young, and I was sure he was going to be one of life's champions in spite of all he had endured. Samvel was just 19 years old.

---

[17] *Nagorno-Karabakh: Azerbaijan Announces Capture of Major City.* Deutsche Welle. Online at: https://www.dw.com/en/nagorno-karabakh-azerbaijan-announces-capture-of-major-city/a-55536491

CHAPTER 10

On Volunteering

In bustling Yerevan, I had a hard time finding proper venues to interview my subjects. After making some phone calls, I finally got hold of a room where no music and no one wandering in could interrupt my conversation with the next interviewee—another Samvel (A.). When we met, Samvel was still shuffling along haltingly, as he was on crutches. We asked for tea and started the interview. Samvel's thoughts were still scattered all over the room. I waited patiently and let him take his time to focus.

I went off to the war on September 28thand was bound for Mataghis with my mates. We stayed there until October 4th. It was a disaster: there were no professional soldiers with us. They accompanied us as far as Mataghis and then skedaddled. I wasn't surprised, as I'd also been in the Four-Day War of April 2016. I'd witnessed no end of betrayals during that war as well. However, I realized that many of the other volunteers were experiencing for the first time that that's how it goes. Seeing the commanding officers leaving them in the lurch put a lot of them off, and they had major questions about whether they'd been wise to join up.

For the next few days, we walked through the woods in the Talish district without knowing what territory was still held by the Armenians. We had no maps and not a single walkie-talkie; we had rifles but not enough ammo to go around. They were fighting us mainly from the air, with drones. We wanted to move to another position, but before we could, we got word that the soldiers at the front were about to retreat. There was an Azeri saboteur squad on their tail, though. So we had to change our plans and make preparations to join the guys on the front line and counter-attack. Job done, and then we had dinner with the Fourth Battalion in Talish. Altogether, we were a band of a hundred men, including the injured. The rampart of the bunker we saw there looked all kitted out for soldiers to hold out in, but when we went to ask what our next mission was, we found the bunker itself abandoned. There literally was not a single commander willing to stay at our side.

Never mind our discouragement and disappointment; we had to fall back from there. There was only one guy who vaguely remembered where to find the road. We went up the hill toward Eghnikner. The road was full of barriers, challenging to climb over. On the way, some soldiers even attempted suicide, but we urged each other on to the hospital. We had a bite to eat and stayed there overnight. The next day, heavy bombardments started. Again, some soldiers were severely injured, the senior officers didn't hesitate to run away from the battlefield, and once again, we were left alone. We started plodding toward Stepanakert, going through many battles, many betrayals, and many disappointments along the way.

After the ceasefire agreement, Armenian society polarized into two camps: those who entirely justified Prime Minister Pashinyan's decision to end the war so soon and those who believed what he had signed was tantamount to an act of capitulation. Most of the time, when I talked to pro-Pashinyan people (simply because I was open-minded about understanding their position), I found their main argument had to do with the betrayals on the battlefield. I would hear: "What could Pashinyan do if the officers refused to fight?" or, "Pashinyan sent the conscripts and volunteers to war, but he couldn't get the professionals to put up a fight and not leave their men behind on the battlefield." Naturally, I found this a weak argument and one that had nothing to do with the premature outcome of the war, but it was true that our soldiers had in many cases been stabbed in the back. Samvel was not the only man stating this case. Nevertheless, we also had great commanders and military professionals who did fight and stood by their men. Most of them, in fact, had given up their lives for the sake of others. So it would be unfair to talk only about betrayals when most officers had actually fallen on the battlefield beside their men.

We decided to come back to Armenia and join a still-functioning group of rangers, with whom we would fight to the death. During a war, I knew it all came down to what commanding officer you had. Maybe I could make wise decisions for myself, I thought, but I didn't want to take responsibility for others. And, to be honest, I wanted a professional to be with us and show us what to do to stay alive. Unfortunately, though, we didn't make it to Yerevan. On our way, the military police stopped us and took us to Askeran. On October 12th, we were already at the front in Hadrut and had to endure more battles. In them, I assumed the role of a commander. We ended up in a blockade and had an injured man with us. So I ordered my group to leave me behind with the wounded soldier while the rest of them made good their escape from the blockade. With the injured man and two others, I headed off down a hazardous road. I had his back, but the shooting was getting more intense. We had to walk slowly and very carefully.

At some point, I got injured. The bullet entered the sole of my foot and went out through my belly. I rolled into the bushes and stayed there for several minutes. One of the soldiers with me continued walking with the limping guy, and the other one came over my way. He dug a hole under a fence, pulled me through to the other side, and started bandaging my wound to stop the intense bleeding. He was also a volunteer, a smaller guy than me, and there was no chance he could carry me. He was married and had two children, with the third on the way. I managed to convince him to abandon me and save his own life for their sake. He did leave, but he came back again. As I was trying to convince him to get away, his wife phoned him. And at that moment, it was apparent to him that he had to go.

I was still having to bring Samvel constantly back into the moment because on that interview day, his thoughts were somewhere far away. We agreed after a while to call it a day and carry on a week later, over at his place. So it was that I arrived in Nor Hachn and met Samvel at his apartment. He was a different man, feeling more comfortable in his skin and perhaps also safer. Once we'd reviewed where we'd broken off the story the last time, Samvel went on.

I just stayed in that open field for around four days. Ravenous, and my condition was getting more critical by the day. I was struggling to keep my eyes open. Right when I was about to give out, a pomegranate fell on the ground right next to me. I grabbed and ate it. Don't ask me how, but that pomegranate gave me so much strength that I managed to inch forward on my belly until I reached an abandoned house. I couldn't find anything to drink there but vodka. I poured it on my wound and rebandaged it. There were some dried fruits there that I gobbled up to survive.

Realizing there was a truck parked in front of the house, I thought of escaping in it. I only barely reached the steering wheel, turned the key, and it roared into life. For sheer joy, I didn't wait for the engine to warm up, and I just stepped on the gas. The truck smashed straight into an iron fence. I knew I had to brake, but my left leg wasn't functioning. I couldn't find the right pedal as I fumbled for the brake. The truck didn't stop and tumbled down the hill. I spent another couple of hours extricating myself from the wreck. The window wouldn't break, and the door was too heavy for me to open. I have no idea how, but ultimately I managed to clamber out.

I could only crawl downhill. After I got out of the truck, I spotted another house. I knew there were already Azeri soldiers in Hadrut, and most probably in that house as well, but I was hungry, so I took the risk and entered the house from an open window. I found some grub, tucked in, and heard footsteps. There was a small table in the room, and I managed to crawl under it and cover myself with the tablecloth. They entered, took something, and left. I waited until I could hear no more voices. But apparently, they'd realized I was there and were waiting. Finally, one of them jabbed under the table with a shovel. They caught sight of me and started shooting, and in the end, got hold of me.

After the enemy caught me, they dragged me left and right, and I tried to explain that I had a massive wound and that I had no way of harming them. But they spoke no Russian, and we couldn't communicate at all. They'd already rustled some sheep from that house, but now, they let the sheep go so they could tie me up with the rope instead. As I approached the car, hopping on one leg, one of their soldiers noticed my cross necklace, took his knife out, and tried to slaughter me. Another man stopped him and reminded him about the reward they would get for me. They would get 100 dollars for my head, or even more if I were delivered alive, as far as I understood. On the way, they started torturing me while burning my hands and ordering me to say bad words about Pashinyan while filming me. After we arrived [this was still in Hadrut], they made me walk to the fifth floor, where a nurse had a look at my wound, which had gotten bigger and more suppurating from being out in the sun for seven days.

Samvel didn't hide his disappointment. He told me that when he incurred his injury, his mobile phone was still working, so he called the emergency services, and they told him to fire shots into the air. But his rounds inevitably ran out, and obviously so did his hopes of being rescued.

They asked me if I could speak Azeri. Of course, I couldn't, and they started beating me up because they wanted me to communicate with them in Azeri. And then, out of the blue, they accused me of being a military professional and punched me in the face. I got my army identity card out and told them to open it up and read it. We argued about everything. They were convinced the Russians were fighting for us against them, and I sought to explain to them that it wasn't true. Finally, after the interrogation, they removed my blindfold and made a video of me,[18] promising they would send it to the Red Cross and other international organizations. After keeping me at that military base in Hadrut, they took me to Baku the next day. It was on the way there that the real trials began.

---

[18] A video of Samvel was disseminated on the internet in which he was ordered to curse Prime Minister Pashinyan (in Russian). Online at: https://www.facebook.com/watch/?v=2736504066604390

By the time we reached Baku, I was half a man. Besides the beatings, they'd pierced me with a metal skewer so often that I couldn't feel my other leg. It was here that they burned my hands. One of the soldiers turned a lamp on and ordered me to keep my eyes on it until we reached Baku. Nothing could satisfy them or make them think of stopping the torture. We had to stop the car so many times on the way for them to drag me out, beat me to a pulp, spray something on my eyes and then continue the drive. I had to say, "Karabakh is Azerbaijan," and they burned my fingers. They would torture me and laugh incessantly.

I chose the title *Sadistic*[19] *Pleasures* for this book to reflect the many stories I was told in which the Azeri soldiers would enjoy the pain of their Armenian captives. Many of my friends thought this odd because they associated the word "sadism" with perverse sexual gratification, but actually, the word also means extreme physical cruelty or enjoying the pain of others, such as the enjoyment the Azeris derived from hurting their Armenian captives. Yet the most cynical part was that after humiliating the Armenians in so many different ways, they would consider themselves kind and even set about guilt-tripping their prisoners.

We finally got to Baku. First, they took me to the hospital, took readings from all my vital organs, and concluded that everything was "fine." The next destination was the secret service building. There, they told me that because I was injured, they would refrain from roughing me up. I shot back that I would tell them the

---

[19] According to the Collins English Dictionary, "sadism" means the gaining of pleasure or sexual gratification from the infliction of pain and mental suffering on another person.

same thing anyway, with or without beatings. I stayed there for ten days with Saro. They humiliated Saro without any sense of humanity. Saro knew no foreign languages, which unleashed the Azeris' brutality. We had no hope of returning, but in the early days, they told me that two of their men were being held captive in Armenia and the Armenian Government would exchange them for us. In the secret service building, they would interrogate us from 5 a.m. until late at night. It was easier for me because I'd been on my own when they captured me. So, no matter what they did, I would tell them they had to believe my account.

They didn't tire of asking me about Khojaly. During some questions, they applied electric shocks, burning my hands again. As they looked inside my military identity card, they saw that I'd also participated in the war in April 2016. They wanted to make a video of me saying that we'd fired at peaceful civilians during the April war. I told them that it wasn't true, but they didn't care. I didn't have any choice about it anyway. After several days in the secret service building, I was taken to Baku Prison and was held in a cell with four other Armenians until the end of my captivity.

The prison was near the Caspian shore and an airport. I shared a cell with Ruben [the same Ruben as was in Narek N.'s group], Valer [who had shared a cell with Arega's husband Edvard until his death], and Sasha. Sasha made the days difficult for us. He acted as if he'd lost his mind. When the Azeri guards opened the door, we were commanded to shout and repeat, "Karabakh is Azerbaijan." Sasha would say something else, though, and then babble on in Azeri. The guards would go crazy; they would come and pull his hair, tell him they would kill him if he didn't stop right away. We did a lot for Sasha: washed his clothes, went without some of our portions to let him have more food, we would help him shower. We respected him for his age. But he was a very ungrateful man. In the end, he cursed us and told us that he wished we stayed there until the end of our lives. We couldn't work out if he was acting or really had gone crazy.

Samvel chuckled.

The Azeri guards took Valer out of the cell and told us that he was being packed off home—not that I believed a word of it. In the beginning, the Red Cross were visiting Ruben, then after some days, Sasha and then me. When I met the Red Cross, our first question was whether Valer had duly got "home" and how Saro was doing. Valer was still in Baku Prison, they said, in another cell. And according to the Red Cross, Saro was getting better. I wrote a letter to my parents telling them that everything was manageable. My dad also wrote me a letter, but I never received it. There were many Armenian captives in Baku Prison. We could communicate by banging on the wall. For example, if we gave four knocks, they would reply with either three or four; that was how we worked out that there were either three or four Armenians in that cell. We were in cell number 69 and communicated with the cell where Garik was being held.

The most unbearable days were when I was in the cell, and the war was still going on. I felt powerless. When they took Shushi, there was joy and celebration in the whole prison. Even the menu was changed for the entire day. They opened the windows for the first time and gave us cigarettes. It was bloody miserable for all of us.

Closer to the time of our repatriation, many Russian officers started visiting us in the cell. The Azeri guards would let us open the window and get some lungfuls of fresh air every time the Russians were about to visit us. We understood that our chances of returning were improving. In the last few days, they opened the door and told us they had good news. I still remember their names: Ravshan, Fuad—who was the boss—and Zaur. They said they wanted to 'stay friends' with us when we got home! On December 14th, we arrived in Armenia. But there were still many Armenian captives in Baku Prison, and it was only 44 of us who returned home in exchange for the two murderers of Smbat Tsakanian.

CHAPTER 11

All in Exchange for All

My stay in Armenia was coming to an end, but I was keen to interview the Tsakanian family. It was thanks to this family's generosity, understanding, and care that many Armenian POWs and civilians had returned home, including Arineh, Arega, Sasha, Vahé, the two Nareks, and the two Samvels, and many others besides. It was not an easy decision for them to agree to release their son's murderers.

> It was July 2, 2014. I was waiting for Smbat. He didn't come. I called him, but—very unusually of him—he didn't answer the phone. I asked Mekhak [Smbat's father] if he would stop on his way to Karvachar to see if everything was alright with Smbat. Then I called my daughters; I thought maybe he was just staying the night there. On July 4th, Mekhak went after Smbat; he opened the door of the house that Smbat was supposed to be in, but no one was at home. I called everywhere; no one had any news. I called the police. The whole village went out searching for Smbat. His dead body was found on July 16th.

On July 4th, an Azeri reconnaissance and saboteur squad of three men—Dilgam Asgarov, Hasan Hasanov, and Shahbaz Guliyev—crossed the border armed with rifles and ammunition. They kidnapped the 17-year-old Smbat Tsakanian and later murdered him, leaving his body in the woods in the Shahumyan district.

> I was at my daughter's place when I was told of Smbat's death. They didn't let me see his body. We held

his funeral without me being allowed to caress my son's body for the last time. For seven years, I refused to accept he had actually been killed until I was able to watch the documentary coordinated by Larisa Alaverdian. In the film, I could see his body. Although it was covered with plastic sacks, I realized it was my son.

When we watched the documentary about Smbat's death together, I saw many gunshot wounds on his body. Item 6 on the agenda of the OSCE Human Dimension Implementation Meeting in 2017, held from September 11th to 22nd, concerned Smbat's case. After killing Smbat Tsakanian, the three saboteurs managed to kill Sargis Abrahamyan and fatally wound Kariné Davtyan on the Vardenis-Karvachar Highway on July 11th; the gun used in that double attack was traced to Hasanov. Fortunately, the Armenian Armed Forces managed to track down all three of them. However, during the arrest, Hasanov put up resistance and was shot. The two others were captured and sentenced: to life imprisonment in Askerov's case and 22 years in Guliyev's.[20]

> These three Azeris had been there since early 2014, but the Armenians hadn't been able to catch them. As Smbat and Serob [Smbat's brother] were harvesting walnuts together, the three of them had them under observation. Serob had to return home the next day, but Smbat told him not to wait till then. So, as soon as Serob left him and Smbat set off home on his own, these murderers abducted my son. At their trial, the two saboteurs admitted all their crimes. I looked them in the eyes in court and demanded to know what my

---

[20] OSCE Human Dimension Implementation Meeting, 2017. Online at: https://www.osce.org/files/f/documents/8/4/346056.pdf

son had ever done to them. As Askerov was sentenced to life imprisonment, he started weeping and asking to be tortured like Smbat was, and begged to be killed, just not to be in the position of a prisoner.

Of course, I was not surprised to read about the Republic of Azerbaijan encouraging such crimes prompted by ethnically-motivated hatred toward Armenians. Their government did put effort into justifying the crimes of the murderers, as described above, by insisting that the criminal group had "peacefully" entered the territory of Artsakh because they "wanted to visit the graves of their relatives." However, none of the members of that group had been born in or ever lived in the territory that they entered illegally in 2014. Yet they still insisted this was the case. If so, then there was a legal procedure in place whereby they could apply to visit the graves. In fact, many Azeri journalists, human rights activists, and other figures have visited Artsakh by going through these procedures. Even if they wanted so desperately to lay flowers on their relatives' graves that they couldn't wait to go through the legal formalities, there was no need to pack three 7.62 mm Kalashnikov assault rifles fitted with silencers, three 9 mm Makarov pistols with silencers, two daggers, several F-1 hand grenades, and other ammunition, and two Sony camcorders, one of which was found to contain video footage of critical infrastructure, military bases, and the like.[21] And, oops, they forgot the flowers...

---

[21] UN General Assembly Security Council. 2019. Memorandum from the Ministry of Foreign Affairs of the Republic of Artsakh on Azerbaijan's international responsibility for particularly serious crimes committed in Artsakh by Azeri citizens Shahbaz Guliyev and Dilham Askerov. Online at: https://www.un.org/sites/un2.un.org/files/webform/s74_2.pdf

I started getting a flood of phone calls asking us to agree to the freeing of this pair of murderers. The Armenian authorities explained that it was the only price we were able to pay to free all the POWs and civilians from Baku Prison. It was a tough decision for me, but I could imagine how their families were mourning, as I had for my Smbat. In the beginning, I couldn't agree to it. Then I decided we must exchange these two for all of them. So I let them return the murderers of my son to Azerbaijan. Actually, when the guys visited me to thank our family for freeing them, I felt as if my Smbat had returned home.[22] All of them were Smbat to me. I don't regret my decision; watching the young men being brought back from death made my life more meaningful. Even so, they were supposed to return all of them.

The Tsakanian household was one of the warmest and most hospitable places I visited during the whole month of March 2021. I would like to express my deepest gratitude to Mekhak and Kariné Tsakanian, the parents of Smbat Tsakanian.

A gentle reminder of the current state of affairs:

…Whereas paragraph eight of the ceasefire agreement provides that "exchange of prisoners of war, hostages and other detainees, as well as the remains of the fatalities, shall be carried out"; whereas it was agreed by the parties concerned that the return of captives would be carried out on the principle of "all in exchange for all…" whereas Azerbaijan still holds Armenian prisoners of war and has allegedly made new prisoners, including civilians, after the official end of hostilities; whereas it is dif-

---

[22] PanArmenian.net: *Armenian Soldiers Visit Tsakanian Family after Return from Baku.* 2021. Online at: https://www.panarmenian.net/eng/news/289696/Armenian_soldiers_visit_Tsakanian_fa mily_after_returning_from_Baku

ficult to precisely draw up the number of remaining prisoners and captives, due to the high number of missing persons and the lack of cooperation from the Azeri side, but it would include 69 people whose captivity Azerbaijan admits, 112 people about whom Azerbaijan did not provide any information, and 61 people whose captivity Azerbaijan categorically denies, but about whom there is concrete evidence to the contrary...[23]

---

[23] European Parliament. 2021. *Motion for a Resolution*. Online at: https://www.europarl.europa.eu/doceo/document/B-9-2021-0281_EN.pdf

CHAPTER 12

The New Life We Can Build out of This Story

It was already midnight when I took my leave of the progressive youth of downtown Yerevan. I've lived in Germany for three years now, and no amount of social progressiveness could make me blush anymore. However, as I left, I felt confused and upset. But upset at whom or what? We were living through the most shameful era of our national history. I opened the door of my guest apartment and hoped no one was still awake. I put the kettle on and sat for another two hours in that welcome silence. My thoughts were like a rushing wind, making me feel I was unable to withstand this brutal reality.

The taxi drew up at my destination. I hurried to find the appointment room and get ready for the interview, this time in the western city of Gyumri. I gulped down my third coffee of the day and went down to the entrance to meet him. There he was: a tall guy with big eyes and a broad grin. I didn't have to ask if he was Garik:[24] he approached me and cracked a joke, a dead giveaway that someone's from Gyumri. As we took our seats in the room, excitement filled the air. I had been waiting for a long time to listen to his story.

When the war started on September 27th, I told my parents I'd volunteered to join up. If it had been me who was a full-time soldier when war had broken out,

---

[24] As this interviewee wanted to stay anonymous, I gave him the pseudonym Garik. The other names he mentioned are also fictitious in this account, as many of the subjects are still in captivity.

I would be very grateful for volunteers supporting me on the battlefield. I was straight off to the army base in Gyumri. After being handed our uniforms, we were imagining we would get some basic training before heading out to Artsakh. Nothing of the sort. We twiddled our thumbs until October 3rd before being dispatched to Artsakh to support our soldiers as best we could. But not every soldier was lucky enough to be properly equipped before heading to the battlefield. I was among the less fortunate: I had no bulletproof vest when the war broke out, and not during it, either.

I was not in the least surprised, as Garik was not the first guy I'd spoken to who had taken part in the war without proper equipment. It made me loathe our government all the more, as they had sent these young men off to protect our motherland without putting in an ounce of effort for their protection. Who knows how many lives were snuffed out on the battlefield just for want of flak jackets?

I called my sister and informed her that I was off to Artsakh with around 359 soldiers. On the journey, I sat by the window. As we arrived, I somehow recognized the place and reckoned it was Jabrayil Base. The closer we got, the surer I was that it was the same place where I'd completed my military service a couple of years earlier. We had orders to entrench around 25 km from the main army base. The first day was relatively calm; from the second day onwards, we were constantly making life-or-death decisions.

He started the story with a big, winsome smile. He was special, this one. He kept repeating: "When's the book coming out? I don't want my parents to know I told you every last detail. We worry about the rest of the captives, you know. Can't you hold off publishing until all the boys are home?" I could make no promises, not because I was a natural pessimist, but because, having heard so many of the POWs' stories and Aliyev's pronouncements, it was apparent to me that he had not the least intention of freeing all of the detainees.

> The bombardments and the chaos started at one and the same moment. So we had to move on from one unit to another, on foot. On the way, some of the guys did a bunk. The commanding officers were not at their posts; most of us had no idea where we were or what to do. We dug in and waited for further developments. There were ten men in the position where I was. Some of the soldiers were without bulletproof vests or had no walkie-talkie. As evening descended, there was panic among the soldiers. Everyone started shooting every which way; we even noticed a light in the middle of a field, and we started aiming at it. We had no idea they might have been Armenians. Then a soldier walked toward me. I asked if he was an Armenian, but he didn't answer. I started shooting in his direction, and then he said he was Armenian. I asked him some questions to be sure he was telling the truth.

If I saw Garik on the streets, I would think of him as the essential artist, a shrinking violet. He had this cherubic face, a delicate complexion, seemingly too refined to fight. But on the battlefield, men like him can become tougher than country boys, more resilient, and more inured to death and killing. This realization made me question my understanding of humanity.

> As the days passed, the situation got even worse. On October 5th, we were under heavy attack. For one thing, I felt the drones flying over me, and for another, we had to do something about our miserable conditions.

It was raining, and we had no shelter. So, with the drones buzzing overhead, we set to digging a foxhole, as we had to have somewhere to shelter in. There was just one commander with us, and he was completely in the dark as to the progress of the war. The rest of the commanders were much better informed. On that day, suddenly, rumors spread that Azeri forces had broken through the Armenian lines and were approaching us. The same stories were also spread on October 4th.

We readied ourselves to engage the enemy. I was tasked to reload the weapons of soldiers whose magazines ran out during firefights. However, we saw no Azeri troops approaching us. On October 6th, as the drones kept bombing our positions, we took refuge under the shelter we had built. It was made of concrete slabs, with a frame consisting of iron construction materials. As the drone bombarded us, this whole concrete contraption collapsed, leaving us stuck under it. That is: me, Erik, and Sevak. Somehow, Erik and I managed to crawl out, but Sevak was pinned beneath the full weight of the structure. We started digging as madly as dogs dredging a ditch to find bones. I scrabbled as fast as I could, the drones bombing us from all sides as we worked. My mates came over to help. It was unreal. We were trying to save our comrade's life as a shot from a drone could have killed any of us any second. We managed to grab Sevak from under the heavy building materials. We reconstructed the dugout, but we now knew we couldn't rely on it to hold firm."

We were planning on walking several kilometers to get food, to where there was a special unit that also gathered the corpses of the Armenian fallen. The idea was that these corpses would be transferred from that muster station to Armenia, which never occurred. The commanders miscalculated, left the bodies behind, and did a runner.

I immediately thought of a particular soldier listed as missing since the middle of the war. He was from my village. As Garik told me many corpses had been left behind, I caught myself thinking: "Maybe he's one of those left-behind bodies, as he too fought in Jabrayil."

On October 7th, we were watching soldiers at the front fighting the Azeris. As we were waiting in the rear to attack as soon as we received the order, we realized our front line was backing up. We saw how the army gave up the ground and moved backward; still, though, we had no word to attack. We were just waiting there. We could hear the soldiers shouting, pleading for reinforcements. Some of them were running off every which way; others were fighting on at a hilltop where the Azeris had already planted their flag. The situation was getting more out of hand by the minute. On October 8th or 9th, when we actively joined the battle, we realized how blessed we were still to be alive, without even any bulletproof vests. We asked the commanders to resolve this issue, as we wanted to come to our soldiers' aid and join the fight. Nothing was done."

Another reason I found Garik so special was that he was carefully weighed each word he uttered. He laughed a lot, and wasn't averse to the odd joke, but it was never over the top. The war had indeed made him "measure thrice before cutting once." He even carefully timed when to crack a joke to relieve the tension. His intonation and well-judged pauses made the five-hour interview fly by smoothly and pleasantly.

As I mentioned earlier, I'd previously served in Jabrayil. My mother always asks me to bring some pomegranates with me when I visit her. As I arrived on October 4th, I saw a vast pomegranate orchard, and I picked six of the finest. I thought when I returned, I'd give them to mum. During the whole time in Jabrayil, quite apart from the bombardments, we had a job finding water; but food wasn't in short supply. In the evenings, we would sing patriotic songs. Not everything was bleak, you know. Even so, on October 11th, the bombardments drew significantly closer. Our soldiers were still resisting, though.

On October 14th, we got wind that the Azeris were planning to attack. So we stayed up all night, getting ready for the onslaught. At 9 a.m., the drones started bombarding; they were already too close for our liking. It added more panic to the situation, and we were surprised that the Armenians were not doing anything against these drones. The soldiers started thinking of abandoning their position, so I reminded them that we'd come here with a mission. We weren't there to quit when the chips were down. But then we saw the regular army retreating. Although there was no order to move back, staying there would cost more lives. Four of our guys contacted the commanders to ask why they were not ordering us to join the soldiers at the front and put up a fight. Some of the soldiers walked off; others just disappeared. It was chaos.

When the drones attacked us for the third time, the commanders jumped into their jeeps and left us on the battlefield. One of the soldiers called us and told us that we had only five minutes; we had to get the hell out of there or be killed. We had no maps, no proper equipment, and had run out of options. I took the six pomegranates, shared one with my mates, and, stuffing the rest in my pockets, started walking God knows where.

Damn! Almost all the stories had this in common: chaos and commanders scuttling off, leaving the soldiers to fend for themselves. Armenians discussed this issue to the exclusion of all others for the first week after the ceasefire. That week, though, we weren't talking about finding out what had become of these buffoons who'd left teenage boys on the battlefield and thought only of saving their own skins. Naturally, everyone wants to live, especially on the battlefield. But a commander has to be ready to die before his men. Otherwise, he might as well jack it in, go into politics and write patriotic status updates on social media from his upholstered seat in the National Assembly.

> We had an electricity pylon at our backs, and we made it our orientation point. When we lost sight of it, the sun became our orientation point, but that wasn't there for long either, as night was drawing in. It was hellish. We didn't eat for ages. I threw up many times, my leg muscles were cramping, and I couldn't walk any further. We shared another pomegranate between eight of us. Somehow, we managed to get through to one of the commanders by phone to ask what kit we could leave behind, as we had too much stuff with us and very little strength left. He said we could dump everything but our rifles and magazines. So we took our winter coats off. Although it was freezing, we chose to freeze rather than to waste our whole energy on carrying weight.
>
> Before long, I couldn't move a muscle. Erik helped me through the rest of the walk by carrying my rifle. We walked through the night, couldn't get a phone signal, and all we could do was keep slogging on. We met locals, but every time we spoke to some, they told us we had to "walk another 15 kilometers to reach the next village." On the way, people were fleeing in their cars, and even vehicles with empty seats would pass us

without stopping. We tried to flag them down. Even when one car did stop, and we saw it had two free seats, they told us that they had two other people to pick up along the way.

On we went. Along the way, we saw Armenian troops, so I managed to get a drink of water, and then we pressed on again. Soon, we got enough of a signal to call the brother of one of my comrades and asked for a car to get out of that place. Well, the driver was supposed to pick us up, but he bumped into other soldiers on his way to us and had to help them first. In the end, though, those guys did arrive and took us to the village of Tigranavan. We phoned some of our mates and found out that they'd gone in a completely different direction. We had dinner and rested for a few hours at a petrol station.

Around 2 a.m., the bombardments started up again, and we had to get out of there. We started heading for Goris [in Armenia proper] on foot without any helmets or bulletproof vests. We were escaping, and still, they were shooting at us. So many cars were passing by, and hardly any of them even stopped. Only one car did, in fact. They were a couple. They only had three free seats, and it was me and two others who had priority to be given a lift to Goris. On my way, I thought through ways to evacuate the rest of the guys. When we reached the checkpoint on the Artsakh-Armenia border Armenia at Khndzoresk, the military police started giving us hassle and asking why we were there and not on the battlefield. The officials sent the couple back the way they'd come and told them they were not allowed to leave Artsakh. And they took us off to a military base at Tegh Gyugh.

At that base, they accused us of deserting and logged our names in their system. Around 7 p.m., I managed to get through to Erik, and he told me that they were also heading to Tegh Gyugh by bus. It was already October 16th. After Erik had joined us at Tegh Gyugh, we set off for Yerevan. My dad and brother came to pick us up, and we all went to St John's Church to give thanks. One of us went straight home, as he was injured, but the other six of us went to the church, bought crosses, wrote our names on them, left them at the altar, and then went home. I had three pomegranates left when we arrived in Yerevan. I gave one to Erik and the other two to Mum. She didn't so much as know I'd been in Jabrayil; as I gave them to her, I told her they were from Jabrayil.

Garik's story should have ended here, but he decided to rejoin the soldiers voluntarily. Before he resumed the story, I had my fourth cup of coffee. I was wondering whether people would start believing in God again in such circumstances, with hope ebbed away. Then I would catch myself and be so angry at myself for having such odd thoughts in the middle of a serious interview. The aroma of the coffee relaxed the atmosphere again; I felt he was ready to share more.

On November 26th, Hayk phoned to ask if I wanted to join the guys for a short mission, to protect some of our positions. I agreed, got my kit together, and joined the group on November 27th. This time, I was lucky enough to have a bulletproof vest. We thought we would be going to Lachin [where the Armenia-Artsakh corridor was established at the ceasefire shortly afterward], but after one night, we found ourselves somewhere in Khtsaberd. Our platoon consisted of 62 soldiers. There wasn't much for us to do. We had to walk about to find water, get food, and control a chosen position.

At first, we had a commander, who told us what our task was, but then he buggered off. We were already deep in the mountains and had to collect firewood and keep the fire from going out. The whole platoon was divided into patrols. I had a 12-man patrol, and as six of us sat by the fire, the other squad of six would walk 20 kilometers to get food for us all. On December 1st, we found out that the village we walked through to reach our position had been surrendered to Azerbaijan.

The days were passing by, and nothing was changing. We'd been told that we would only be there for two weeks; the fortnight came and went, and no one showed up to relieve us at post. On December 13th, we had a phone call out of the blue and were told we had only five hours to leave the area, as it was not under Armenian control anymore. We started packing up and walking without knowing where we were going. It was getting dark, and we had to reach a position where some Armenian commanders were supposed to meet us and conduct us back to Armenia. We reached the rendezvous, only to find that no one was there. We forged ahead and kept calling the same number back, but no one was answering, and there was not a soul waiting for us. Already at five minutes past midnight on December 14th, we reached the spot where the Azeri soldiers were waiting for us.

I wasn't sure what to make of this. It smelled like an outright betrayal. Someday, the things I'd heard and witnessed would drive me insane. But this wasn't a game anymore. As soon as I'd seen the viral video of those 62 soldiers filing off to Baku Prison, I'd known someone must have betrayed them. And that someone was Armenian, singular or plural. The questions that would plague Garik for the rest of his life were whether the rest of the platoon would ever return, whether he would ever know whose voice that had been on the phone, and why no one had turned up to meet them at the rendezvous. He deeply believed they would all make it back; I didn't, frankly.

> We never thought this could happen to us. We kept scanning the horizon for the vehicle that was supposed to meet us. One of the soldiers, who'd left ahead of the party to get food together, had already been captured by the Azeri soldiers. When we bumped into them, we saw there was no point in putting up a fight: we were totally unprepared, only half as well-armed as they were, and besides, there were more than 150 of their soldiers, and we were only 62, split up into smaller groups.
>
> So they called each of us to come up, lay down weapons, and wait until everyone was disarmed—after which they promised to "take us to the Russian peace-keepers." We didn't even discuss among ourselves whether we were going to do it or not; we just shuffled forward, one after another. I was the last one after Erik in our group. There were still some stragglers arriving at the scene, and so started all over again. Finally, an Azeri general arrived and told us that we were "in Azerbaijan." as the territory was under their control. It turned out that the Armenian Government knew, and still they had sent us there.

I wonder what that latter-day Che Guevara, our dashing leader who imported the Velvet Revolution to Armenia in 2018, would say if he ever reads this book. Back in 2018, we took to the streets en masse with passionate chants of, "Democracy! Democracy!" And now? Traumatized, lost generations, a polarized society, an economy on life support, collapsed institutions, soldiers missing in action, and nobody-knows-quite-how-many POWs. Our "Velvet" Revolution might yet slip its gloves off and reveal an iron fist, but perhaps that would at least save us from dying out.

They tied our hands and ordered us to walk, threatening that they would shoot anyone who tried to escape. Off we went. On the way, they made a video of us, where we had to say that Karabakh belonged to Azerbaijan. In the morning, they made us carry some of their stuff, and we kept walking. In my mind, I was playing out three scenarios: either they really would "hand us over to the Russian peacekeepers," or they would finish us off somewhere, and the final possibility was that we would end up in captivity. We had to climb up an extremely narrow road, with deep gorges on both sides. On the way, one of the Azeri soldiers told me that in the 1990s, the Armenians had killed his father, and he was there to take the moral high ground: that although our soldiers had killed his dad, he and the rest wouldn't kill any of us. They posed for lots of selfies with us and jabbered in their language while we walked on.

We reached a village in Hadrut district; they took us to a bombed-out library. They made us kneel down in three rows, and we waited. Here, we grasped—or at least I worked out—that the scenario of meeting the Russians was out of the question. Then they divided us into three groups and made us sit in KAMAZ trucks. Our hands were still tied, and they told us to wait a bit in the truck "until the Russians arrived." It had already been 39 hours, we had had no sleep, and we were drained. We fell asleep in the truck. As we arrived in Baku, we jumped out of the back one after the other, and each time a guy jumped off, the Azeri soldiers would start beating him. I was the last one; the moment I made a move to jump off, they kicked me in the face, and the blood was all over me. They separated us into cells, and since that day, I haven't seen many of the Armenian soldiers again.

That is why I hated it when people said, "the war was over." The war was not over, and it is still not. The question was whether it would ever be. How could the war be 'over' when 62 soldiers were captured after the ceasefire agreement? Did the ceasefire agreement mean peace was guaranteed or not? I'm wary of revolutions, especially when the velvet gloves come off them.

At first, we were held in the military police building, where we couldn't expect much courtesy. They were beating us every single day there. They wouldn't even go through the motions of interrogating us; they would just open the door and set about us with a police baton or a heavy iron chain. We were so exhausted, hungry, and thirsty, and we had no hope of resting any time soon. We had to stand throughout the first two days. Two days into the ordeal, though, one of the Azeri supervisors let us have a sip of water and rest a bit. Then they did a roll-call and placed us in a vehicle to transfer us to Baku Prison, where conditions were much better. I had to take the clothes off the other Armenian soldiers, collect them in a bag and take them to a small room. I had four bags full of Armenian soldiers' clothes. I could see some of my comrades' clothes among them, and so it was that I realized that all of us had ended up here at Baku Prison.

As I got back to the cell that day, an Azeri soldier punched me right on the nose and broke it. I'd done nothing. I guess it was just because I was Armenian. He taunted me with how we Armenians believed in the ancient "myth" of Tigranes the Great [r. 95–55 BC]. We were being beaten because they deeply believed

Armenians had killed their relatives back in the 1990s. After some more blows to the face, they left us there in the cell. There were five of us waiting to see what would happen next. As it turned out, they came back and doled out some blankets.

In the room, there were five beds and four pillows. The only thing we had to do was to say, "Karabakh is Azerbaijan" every time someone entered the cell. There was also a window in the cell, with iron bars on it. Through it, we could see a big exercise yard, surrounded by very high walls, topped with a barbed-wire fence. I even saw a swastika on the walls. The room had 78 flagstones, one table, and three chairs. Each mealtime, we would draw the table and three chairs up to my bed. Inside the cell, there was a toilet with a bath. When we opened the window from time to time, we would hear the whirr of a helicopter.

Our cell was number 68. When the guards brought us our breakfasts, we caught the names of some of the dinner ladies delivering to the corridor, including Lyuba, Sulfiya, and Eva. The cell walls were allegedly yellow but had turned filthy long since. There were also eight mattresses in the cell, and one of them was sodden with bloodstains. To start with, we felt miserable about having to yell out, "Karabakh is Azerbaijan," but then we found something positive about even that. You see, we strained to hear how many times the slogan was called out down the corridors, and so we managed to count the number of cells holding our comrades. At one point, we worked out it was either 12 or 13 cells full of Armenians at Baku Prison.

The first interrogation was on day ten. On the way to the interrogation room, I was forced to look down so as not to see anything along the way. They draped everything around me so that I couldn't see much. They asked if I was related to any high-ranking Armenian official and if I had any family members in Russia. I also had to lie through my teeth and say that I hadn't fought and that I'd spent the whole war at the army base in the village of Voskehask. Then they started asking questions about my dad: if he had participated in the first war. They also asked whether I had been to Jabrayil. I told them that I had a call-up from the military police, and they'd told me that if I didn't join the war effort, they would sentence me to seven years of imprisonment. The Azeri officials started telling me—truthfully—how we'd been betrayed and how the Armenian Government had been perfectly well aware it was having us sent to a location under Azeri control. When they carted Aram off for interrogation, they beat him up even on the way there, but I couldn't understand why. He was spattered in blood, terrified of the electric shocks and other tortures he had to undergo during interrogation.

Later, when I returned to Germany, I was long occupied with finding a rationale for this case. The pain was enough to drown in. True, Garik laughed and joked, but even his wisecracks were like a stealthy stab in the back. I kept in contact with him, texting him from time to time. He was still the same: clearly confused. There is so much darkness to this story.

It was my birthday on December 26th. The supervisors entered the cell, made us put black trousers on, handcuffed and blindfolded us, and led us out. We thought we might be going home, but it turned out to be just another interrogation process. They told me that the folks in Armenia had written us off for dead. We were charged with "terrorist activity," which meant we would stay in Baku Prison forever. We even signed a testimony "confessing" that we were terrorists after an interrogation by Mehman Babayev. Finally, they opened the door on December 31st and asked Karen if he would like to return home. Karen said he would, and his supervisor assured him and all of us that soon, we would be going back. He wished us a happy new year.

Incidentally, he was the only Azeri who had anything good to wish us. We were ordered to put lights out at 11 p.m., and on the stroke of midnight, they started yelling, seeing in the new year with fireworks, and then we all got to sleep. But every day, our hope increased that we would come back.

Karen and I always thought of writing our prison memoirs when we returned. We even had some working titles, such as *The Positive Sides of Negativity*, as we all found there were many positive aspects to captivity. *Going After a Dream Has Its Price* was our runner-up title, as Karen had dreamt a lot about getting a breather from his family and having time for himself. The last option was *A Game of Shadows*, as we would make shadowplay images on the wall when we had nothing else to talk about.

As of the time of this publication in January 2022, Karen remains in captivity.

We had a unique language we used to communicate with the neighboring cell, number 69. Artyom was a drummer, and I could tap out the rhythm they played to cheer on the Shirak football team. When Artyom was sent home on January 28th, and I was also sent home, I told the rest not to play the Shirak beats anymore, so the guys in the other cells would know that the drummer and I had got home already. When Artyom knew he would be going home soon, we gave him the number of our parents to call and tell them that we were doing just fine.

On January 28th, Azeri officials entered our cell, issued us with black trousers, blindfolded us, and took us to the next building, and there we met the Russian general, Muradov. The Azeri official asked for old time's sake to whom Karabakh belonged, and we said to Azerbaijan, and everyone guffawed. As I was about to be repatriated, I lay on my bed and saw a cross left under the bed above me. I concluded there had to have been other Armenians held there before our arrival and resolved I would take the cross back with me for them when I returned.

Maybe it was not a coincidence but God. I grew up a serious girl, but I don't know which is more serious: believing in God or coincidence. Or perhaps they are equally solemn.

After Artyom's return, the Azeri supervisors opened the door to the exercise yard, where we had to get spruced up and also managed to get a breath of fresh air. We felt a breeze and heard the waves of the Caspian. That was the only time we were allowed to go out. Sometimes, we talked to the guards. They would tell us how our grandparents had killed many Azeris, how the Armenians had invented their history, how our flag hadn't even been designed until Levon Ter-Petrosyan became President of Armenia in the 1990s. One of the questions that I found intriguing was when the guards asked when it was in life that I'd first heard of Azerbaijan. I told him it was at school, but to be honest, it was actually while watching the Eurovision Song Contest one year. He would look into our faces and say he could tell that Karen and I wouldn't kill Azeri children—but he had "no doubt Hovhannes and Vahé would."

One night, I had a dream where I was led out of cell number 58. Odd, though, as I was actually in Cell 68. I told the guys about the dream, and they thought it might portend that I'd be heading home on my 58th day of captivity. Well, after precisely that number of days, the guard opened the door—on February 9th—and called my name out: Garik."

I was taken to a room I hadn't been in before. I was given a change of clothes, had a shave, and got freshened up for coming home. When I returned to the cell again, I could see that it was cell number 68 for sure. I took that cross and put it in my pocket. I noted down the phone numbers of Karen and Vahé, put on my Covid mask, hugged the guys, and left with an Azeri official. We were on the first floor, some other Armenians joined us, and we were taken to the airport near the prison. There, we could see Russian flags. They took our handcuffs off, and we boarded the flight to Armenia. I could read the word "Baku" at the airport, so I wasn't dreaming that we were really there.

On landing in Armenia, I didn't know that my family had no idea of my return. They were watching the livestream on Facebook when the Armenian officials read my name out—the first on the list—and they sped off to meet me at the military hospital. Then, the next day, February 11th, the first group of POWs repatriated to Armenia came to visit me in the hospital. I took the cross out of my pocket and asked if they recognized it, and what do you know? Raz said he'd made it. Apparently, he'd been held in the same cell as me in Baku Prison.

I said this time we'd go to St John's Church and leave our crosses there once all the guys were home.

This story paints a vivid picture of the post-war situation in Armenia. The institutions of state had ceased working to such an extent that soldiers were returning from captivity, and there was not a single person responsible for informing their parents of the fact. The parents found out about their sons' return from Facebook. Generally speaking, after the democratic tendency came to power, the country started functioning on Facebook; specifically, Armenian politics became a matter of Facebook livestreams, mainly hosted by the Prime Minister, Nikol Pashinyan.

CHAPTER 13

Fortunately, It Only Lasted Forty-Five Days!

My friend drove me to my next interview appointment, which was in Gyumri. The house was crowded. Although a month had passed since his return from captivity, his family was still welcoming guests, among whom I blended in as just another visitor. It was painful for me to go through all this vicarious suffering time and again, but sometimes the pain brought people together. No wonder Armenians felt astonishingly connected during the war. Pain brought with it the prospect of both defeat and victory. I wanted to know what Tigran (not his real name; he wished to stay anonymous) would tell me. I was wanting to compare his story with Garik's, as they were from the same group. The rest I let the reader judge.

> "I, too, was among the platoon of 62 volunteers in Khtsaberd. As we moved into the theater from Gyumri, the military police officer told us we would only be posted there for two weeks, after which another group of soldiers would come to relieve us of our posts. Well, two weeks had come and gone, but no one had arrived to substitute for us. On December 13th, at around 4 p.m., we received a phone call. The voice on the line told us to walk in a given direction where the Armenians would be waiting to meet us. We started walking and covered around 16 or 17 kilometers before reaching the place given on the phone. Our position was at an altitude of 2,400 meters, the weather was atrocious, and there was snow lying everywhere. We thought maybe the vehicle wouldn't make it up the hill, so we got out and did the remainder on foot. We

were expecting 38 Armenians to be waiting for us, as mentioned in the phone call; instead, we found ourselves facing the Yashma, the Azeri special forces. We had no phone signal to call anyone, and we had no idea the Armenians had already beaten a retreat.

When Garik and I returned from captivity, we found out that we'd been permitted under the agreement to stay in Khtsaberd until 5 p.m.; however, the Armenians didn't call us with that news until 4 p.m. There was no way we could have trogged the 16 or 17 kilometers under those extreme weather conditions in an hour. We didn't reach the final rendezvous point until around 11 p.m. What's more, there was no officer with us; he only showed up on the first day, pointed out where to dig in, and then fled that same day. We decided to appoint a commander from among ourselves, but none of us was familiar with the terrain.

Tigran was one of the most modest interviewees I met during my Armenian trip. I was alone with him and his wife in the room as he started sharing his story. Somehow, I managed to get him to open up; he'd refused any other requests for an interview. He looked altogether willing to speak, but he was deeply worried about the fate of the soldiers still left behind in Baku.

The Azeri soldiers told us to lay down all weapons and promised they would "call the Russian peacekeepers to take us to Armenia." Our disadvantage was that we'd been walking in smaller groups and had no clue that the group ahead of us had already been captured. There were around 150 to 200 soldiers awaiting us. As we arrived, we saw some groups already lined up and the Azeri soldiers pointing their weapons at them. I asked my mate Siso if the Russians were coming to get us, then what was the point of handing them our weapons? Soon, it became clear that our options were limited, as, by that time, the number of Azeri soldiers was mushrooming. We were blocked in to the right and to the left. After laying down our arms, we sat around a fire, waiting for about an hour. There were two fully-armed Azeri soldiers standing behind each Armenian soldier. Because it was already midnight when we arrived, they took us to a cowshed, where we spent the night. We tried to discuss the possible solutions for the whole situation with the guys, but it didn't help much. We had no phones, as the Azeri soldiers had collected them in at the outset.

After the long night, we started walking the following day. The enemy soldiers told us that we would be killed on the spot if we made any sudden movements. We started out in single file. We were in Hadrut, but as we walked through the hills, we left the city behind. On the way, the enemy took that famous video of us and disseminated it on the internet.

What was the point of changing the government if we didn't start the change within ourselves? As I'd watched that video of 62 soldiers heading disarmed into captivity and Azeri soldiers making fun of them, my blood had boiled. I had the feeling someone had just poured salt in my wounds. I expected Armenians living in the heart of Yerevan to pressure the democratically-minded among their politicians for a transparent explanation of the tragedy. Instead, it turned out that people were indifferent. That was when I understood one thing: I was not for revolution, but evolution.

After we reached a heavily battle-damaged town, we ate, and then we headed to Baku in three KAMAZ trucks. It took us around five hours. On the way, they started the beatings with various objects, made fun of us, and shot some more videos. The Azeri soldiers would inflict violence on us, but whenever one of their commanders shouted at them, they stopped acting so childishly. They wanted to know why we were exactly in that position with the military police and who our commanders were. I also expected them to beat us to a pulp once we were in captivity.

After some time, one of the commanders told us that we would be repatriated because they had no reason to keep us in Baku. They'd also realized that we had no information they wanted to have. Already in Baku Prison, the physical violations stopped. Their behavior also gave us more hope: we got food to eat, water to take a shower, and a place to sleep. We hadn't been expecting that. However, the whole situation changed, as, during the interrogation process in the secret service building, they decided to charge us with "terrorist offenses." The reason for this conclusion was that we had been "armed while on their territory." We tried to defend our rights by saying that a terrorist wouldn't be wearing a national-issue army uniform and a rifle with a registered serial number and that we were regular volunteers. We hadn't even known where we were heading; our military vehicles had just taken us to that area and dumped us there. However, we couldn't say much. We just signed a declaration "confessing" that we were terrorists.

I didn't have a law degree, but simple logic was enough anyway to tackle this issue. Well, then, if they all were "terrorists," how come two of them were allowed to return home while the other 60 of them had to be put on trial? Did that mean the two were "less terrorist" than the others, or did it mean that the Russian general was in a good mood the day those two filed past him? All of them had the same status, but only two of them won the lottery. How come? Don't get me wrong: I was only too happy to see Tigran and Garik back home, but still, how come? Never mind the ceasefire agreement; those who lost had only just begun serving their time. It was always that way, especially if one side had been waiting for that very moment for 30 years.

> For the first ten days, I was taken through interrogation procedures, at the end of which, I signed a 'confession' without even knowing what it was. It was in Azeri. After that, almost every day was the same: we ate, smoked, and talked. I stayed in captivity for 45 days. I had no visit from the Red Cross. Fortunately, on January 28th, the guard entered the cell, read my name out, and gave me some clothes. I was only in my underwear, as I'd been ordered to take off my clothes on the day I arrived. So I put my clothes on and followed the guard.
>
> We went to the neighboring building, and as he opened the door, I realized it was the Russian general, Muradov. He told us we would be going home soon. At first, I couldn't believe him, and I wasn't even sure if it was really him until I spotted the Russian flag on his uniform. I got back to the cell and shared the news with the guys. Half an hour later, the guard opened the door again. I followed him. I was handcuffed and blindfolded. Karen joined me. Then we heard a plane landing. When I got home, I called my comrades' parents. Most of my best mates are still in captivity now.

Tigran was challenging to interview. I could see he didn't enjoy it. Nevertheless, being determined to accomplish my project, I set my mind to understanding what had gone on here. Tigran had his wife sitting beside him, and he made sure not to talk about the violations and insults. Even so, this was how he wrapped up the whole conversation: "I felt betrayed. We all did. We protected our land after an attack on it out of the blue, and we were promised we would only be staying there for two weeks. Quite apart from the betrayal, the indifference was devastating."

I wasn't surprised, nor will the reader be by this point. Tigran's family watched the livestream of five captives returning home and saw that one of them was him. Tigran asked the driver if he could call home as he sat in the car. He called his dad and said he had landed at Erebuni Airport. "Maybe they didn't notify our families because otherwise, 62 families would have flocked to the airport when only five guys were actually returning." I begged to differ. Because of the official failure to announce in advance the exact names of the detainees returning home, many families did rush to the airport, hoping to welcome their sons. Maybe even the government got their names from a Facebook post.

The Red Cross was not allowed to visit this group until January 28th, so Tigran didn't meet them. So, for around 45 days, the family of Tigran had no news of him. Fortunately for this family, the silence lasted only 45 days.

CHAPTER 14

Opening the Bible for the First Time

I met Vahé in the library of Heratsi Hospital because it was the only wheelchair-accessible venue locally. Vahé's distinguished voice cut the silence and made his story hang in the air, searing it into the little room long after he was gone. He was from Fantan, a village in Kotayk Province in Armenia proper. Vahé served in the 2020 war voluntarily, hoping to join the soldiers positioned in Eghnikner, as his youngest brother was serving at that position. Instead, he was taken to the 2nd Position in Martuni. Vahé was one of those soldiers who had no bulletproof vest and fought without one until October 19th. After that, he and other Armenian soldiers moved to Fizuli and continued fighting there.

> There were only five of us soldiers and our commander still fighting in Fizuli. The number of attacking soldiers was countless. We had no choice but to dive headlong into the enemy forces. The shelling felt like ceaseless rain. It was a grueling battle. We were exhausted, blockaded to the right and left, and there was nothing for it but to fight until our dying breath. As the brutal fighting was still ongoing, I realized two of my comrades had been killed, and the other three of us were heavily injured. Vacho was the worst wounded: he lost half of his body on the battlefield. He well knew that if we stopped and tried to help him, the Azeri troops would kill all of us in a split second. The price we paid for our survival was unbearably high, as it cost Vacho's life. He blew himself up with a grenade to open a route for us to withdraw. After this tragedy, we immediately retreated, taking with us memories of our fallen brothers.

We walked about two kilometers and joined other Armenian soldiers along our way. As I was also injured, in my head, my mates helped me bandage it. Before I even had a chance to catch my breath, the enemy attacked us again. This time, it was even more savage. There were only 30 of us, and the enemy came at us with around 400 men. I looked right and left; everywhere, there were Azeri soldiers closing in for the kill. We fought for about two hours, and by the end of the battle, only ten of us were left standing. We managed to drag some of the bodies out and bury them, but others were left behind.

He took a deep breath and fell silent. I had the feeling that being the victim was humiliating for him. If I didn't urge him to carry on, he would stop the conversation at any moment. I was very eager to hear his story, as I believed the pain accumulated within him was his and mine; it was ours, as we were of the same people, connected by the same existential threat. People who believe Armenians and Azeris could soon live together as harmoniously as the Germans and the French now do should instead take a bite of reality.

It was already October 24th, the last battle I was able to be part of, as my feet and left arm were heavily injured. Two comrades and I tumbled down into a gorge. There, we bumped into two other soldiers, who were extremely badly wounded. They wanted to help us, but it was obvious they had no chance of survival themselves. The morning of October 25th was the worst time for me. My comrade Levon languished and succumbed to his injuries. I was left with just Edgar. We crawled to safety as bullets whizzed over our heads. The bombardments started out of nowhere whenever they noticed us and tried to thin us out. However, God didn't forsake us. In the evening, we made a plan to climb up an incline, after which we would be on the road. There, we had more chances of meeting up with our forces and being rescued.

But it was so hot, and I had very little energy left; I just fainted. My mate Edgar thought I was dead and had to leave me behind. He was injured as well and had no chance of dragging me up the hill. The next day, I woke up and realized I was completely alone. Mustering all my strength, I resolved to climb the hill at any price. My injured feet were putrefying; I could smell them. Even so, I decided to rescue myself and hoped to live rather than die. I couldn't even understand where all that strength was coming from; maybe it was the basic desire to live. I managed to crawl to the main road, but once I was there, it was obvious that the Armenian army had retreated, and the enemy was controlling the area. It was scorching, and I knew the heat would hasten my death. So I found myself a tree and slept under it.

The pain of his story was tugging my heartstrings. It wasn't just his story, but the whole sight in front of me: he was sitting in a wheelchair, his feet still freshly bandaged, dark circles still all around his eyes, and him constantly stopping to take a deep breath. We were connected through his pain, just like a bridge connecting two neighborhoods of a city, making them a whole. I sensed the pain; it had a distinct taste.

When I opened my eyes, the soldiers were already surrounding me. There were so many of them; I was too weak and didn't have anything left within me for self-defense. I had to leave everything behind, as I didn't have the strength to carry any weight. They thought I was one of their own fighters from Syria. For the first ten minutes, they just couldn't accept I was Armenian. We talked in Russian, and once they were convinced I really was an Armenian, one of their commanders told me that everyone they had captured so far had been put to death. Then he continued, "Today, though, we have orders not to kill anyone we capture, but to take them to Baku."

I told him, "I'm not scared of being killed. If you want to be kind to me, you can kill me now. If you wish me harm, just leave me here. You can come back here tomorrow and find me dead." I had lost pints of blood, and my feet were rotten through and through. If I'd been left there, I was sure I would die by the following day. He looked at me and said he was not minded to kill me. He offered me a cigarette and water and gave me first aid. It was surprising that they had Armenian army uniforms on; the only difference was the red ribbon on the left arm. I managed to observe about ten of them at close quarters, and they all had the same uniform and the same ribbon on. As I realized the sheer number of soldiers on the scene, I didn't care what might happen to me anymore. The commander told me he would send me to Azerbaijan and helped me into a car heading to Baku.

We reached a place where I was handed over to the Azeri army. The Syrian commander told me right away that there wouldn't be any threat to my life as long as I was with him. He added, "As soon as I hand you over to the Azeri commander, mind, I can't be responsible for your life anymore." I was blindfolded as the Azeri officers started interrogating me. The questions were unsurprising to me, as I was painfully aware that I was a captive and the enemy had no reason to be nice to me. I was prepared for anything, and I could imagine that either evil or kindness might be shown to me. They could do anything they wanted at that moment. They started beating me on the way to Baku, stubbing out cigarettes on various parts of my body. I still have some scars from it on my back. Although they could see that my feet were putrefied, it didn't stop them. They stood on them and tortured me both in the car and at the Baku military base.

So if these were not sadistic pleasures, what were they?

During the first five hours of interrogation, I was intensively beaten up. Various guys would just open the door and start on me. It wasn't just with hands or feet; they would use a police baton, an iron rod. They focused mainly on beating me on the feet. They even made me stand; that felt like death. They stood me upright, tied my hands to a pipe overhead, and commanded me to keep standing up straight; otherwise, they would kill me. I could bear that for five minutes, and then I preferred to fall and be killed on the floor rather than dying in an agony like that. They took off all my clothes, except my underwear. I was sweating profusely, and I knew I was close to death. As I fell to the floor, my handcuffs flew open, and so they thought I must be an athlete or a spy, which made them even more violent. The humiliation became twice as intense. They were beating me and making me repeat "Karabakh is Azerbaijan" and dirty slurs about some Armenian commanders. Then they took my phone, which had around ten military photos on it. For each photo, they would inflict excruciating pain on my body. I tried to lie, and I said I wasn't involved in the war and that I'd just been trying to bring the soldiers food but couldn't make it because of the bombardments.

Despite the countless soldiers they'd fielded, many Azeri soldiers had been killed in the battle; so

they would have killed me then and there if I had told
them about my involvement in it. I was interrogated
outside, on a vast square. Two other Armenian captives were with me on that square: one in his mid-for-
ties and the other much older, whom they forced to
beat me up. He understood Azeri, and he would do
whatever he was ordered to. After the interrogation,
they asked me if I could make it to the cell. Of course, I
couldn't. The Azeri officers then asked me if I had ever
seen dogs walking on all fours and commanded me to
walk like a dog while barking. I acted as if I didn't understand, but I either had to do it or experience some
more torture. With my feet being rotten, I sank to my
knees and walked on all fours while barking and so
reached the car. They threw me in the back and took
me to the hospital in Baku.

At the hospital, they carried on beating me even
while helping me shower. There were both good and
bad moments. Once I was presentable, they took me to
the operating theater. The doctors cleaned my body of
all the shell fragments and tried to stop the gangrene
that had started spreading upward from my feet. I had
such a stroke of luck: the doctor treating me, although
an Azeri, had spent time abroad. He didn't let one of
the other doctors amputate and wanted to wait for another three days to see whether he could cure my feet
instead of just chopping them off. Because of that guy,
I didn't end up losing both my legs, but only one foot,
as it had rotted beyond repair in the previous few days.

His eyes were sparkling. He was grateful beyond words to this
doctor and even took a moment to look down and acknowledge
how blessed he was to have the chance to keep his legs. Maybe
one day, the good doctor will read this book: at least he should
know that Vahé appreciates his generosity.

At the hospital, two soldiers guarded me at all times. Even though they knew I was just out of operating theater, for the first five days, specially trained guards would enter my room and start beating me up. They would remind me of the war in the 1990s. I told them I wasn't even born until 1995 and had nothing to do with the first war. But I accepted that, being Armenian, I would have to go through any trial that awaited me in this place. The investigator could speak Armenian, and he would tell me he knew that Armenians were proud of having a five- to seven-thousand-year history. I asked for permission to speak and told him how I'd learned our history was indeed that old and how their national history was not even a hundred years old. Unsurprisingly, they didn't like that kind of answer and slapped me around the chops a couple of times. Then I said maybe I'd got my history wrong, as I was sick of being tortured.

I stayed in the hospital until November 11th; then I was taken to the prison in Baku. On my way, I understood there must be other Armenians being held along with us, as they would scream from pain as they were humiliated. The Azeri officers weren't torturing me anymore, and they even gave me a cellmate, another Armenian called Hovsep. Hovsep was a clergyman, and he, too, was heavily injured. As we arrived at Baku Prison, they removed my blindfold and took me to the fourth floor in a wheelchair. There were around ten to 12 cells on that floor, full of Armenian captives. Our cell was number 62, and I was in a cell with Hayk and Hovsep. I slept in the bed, Hayk and Hovsep on the floor, as it was only designed as a one-man cell.

I had problems walking, so Hayk would always carry me to the toilet, which had no seat. It was a challenge for me to use it. Once, the guard saw Hayk carrying me and helping me in the toilet; he brought a chair to make the conditions more convenient. He even showed some flashes of righteous indignation, as he said we should have asked him for help earlier. So I can't say that everyone hated us or was the same; there were also nice guys mixed in with the mean ones. There was a light in every dark situation I had to go through.

We would wake up at six o'clock every day, eat something and bide our time for lunch. The food was about enough to keep us from fainting. The guards might give some cigarettes, depending on their mood that day. We prayed a lot. As Hovsep was a believer, he would pray constantly. I had never prayed in my life, nor had I had any inclination to open the Bible before. I was a nominal Christian but had no idea about Christianity; I didn't even know how to pray. This now became very shameful to me. I had the feeling that God had sent Hovsep to my cell to help the two of us become closer to Him. Sometimes, we would take leave of reality and would dream of being in Armenia with our families. We learned each other's life stories; it turned out I was the youngest guy, and Hayk and Hovsep were both married already. Hovsep even had a daughter, and Haik had got married just three months before the war started.

One of the greatest lessons I learned during this entire experience was that I hadn't spent enough time with my family. I was always knocking around with my friends, and then I'd been called up to serve in the army, after which I'd worked away from home and never had time for relatives. So, if I had the chance to return home, I promised myself I would spend more time with my parents. Then I also started regretting that I wasn't married yet. So, just like the first time when I was injured to the head, I thought of my family. This second time, as I felt death closing in as a POW, I thought how good it would have been to have at least some progeny to survive me.

On December 12th, the Red Cross visited me. Psychologically, they steeled me for the possibility I would have to stay there through the winter. They didn't utter a word about the likelihood that I'd be going home in two days. They gave me shoes and socks. That day, I called my parents for the first time and told them I'd been captured. I even wrote them a letter, which my parents never received. I'm actually glad they didn't get it, as I wrote too many deeply personal things in it about my feelings, life and death. It was a farewell letter. So it's just as well they never read it.

Vahé was a bit of a philosophical type. He used words thoughtfully and deliberately, and showed himself to be a very calm and understanding young man. It was strange to me: this was already the fifth person I'd interviewed, and none of them wanted revenge, nor had any of them even expressed disgust or hatred toward the Azeris. Isn't it a normal reaction to have negative feelings against a group that humiliates you? Azeri officials condoning violence and discrimination, justifying them on the basis of a single act in the past, and ignoring the rest of the crimes their own side has committed toward hundreds of Armenians can in no way be accepted. The Azeri Government must take responsibility for their silent crimes.

The guard entered the cell on December 14th and told us to shower and get ready. The doctor had a look at my wound and changed the bandages. We were nonplussed. Then the doctor asked if we would like a cigarette. As Hayk said he would, the doctor replied, "In a couple of hours, you can have a smoke in Armenia. Get your stuff together; you're heading home." We thought he was having us on—but then we were ordered to go outside. Hayk carried me down the stairs and helped me into the car that took us to the airport. There were 44 of us captives returning home. I would never wish for anyone to go through the trials I had to endure. I have both positive and negative memories, but the negative ones predominate. The return was life-changing. We were both overjoyed and heartbroken, but the fact was we'd been given a new life.

CONCLUSION

This book is based on witness statements collected from the repatriated Armenians who spent days, weeks, and months in captivity in the enemy's hands. My aim was to document the violations of international humanitarian and human rights law committed by the government of the Republic of Azerbaijan and its military forces toward Armenians: young and old, military forces and civilians, and men and women alike.

As the author of this book and the interviewer behind these stories, I hold my own conclusions about what is happening and what ought to be done about it. As you finish reading these first-hand accounts, I hope I have provided enough information for you to reach your own conclusions and contribute to raising awareness about the brutal human rights violations still taking place against real people.

This book calls for international action against the injustice towards the Armenians who fell into Azerbaijani captivity. These witness statements demonstrate courage and a will to stand for justice. There are still hundreds of Armenians in Azerbaijani custody (an estimated 200 POWs and other captives).[25] Therefore, the fight must be carried on until the very last Armenian returns home and the perpetrators receive and accept punishment for the war crimes committed. Turning a blind eye to Azerbaijan's mistreatment of Armenian POWs during and after the September 2020 war means ignoring the Geneva Conventions (I

---

[25] "It was torturous": Armenian POWs testify to torture in Azerbaijani captivity. 15.09.2021, Armenianweekly.com. Online: https://armenianweekly.com/2021/09/15/it-was-torturous-armenian-pows-testify-to-torture-in-azerbaijani-captivity/

and III).[26] Moreover, leaving the perpetrators unpunished means letting them continue to play with the fates of the remaining Armenian captives still held by the government of the Republic of Azerbaijan.

Based on the stories shared in this book, it is evident that the Azerbaijani forces conducted arbitrary beatings and mistreatment on Armenian POWS and civilians. Indeed, there were cases where the Armenians received medical help or protection from mistreatment. However, the abuse, discrimination, constant beatings with feet, hands, electroshocks, ropes, and degrading anti-Armenian slogans were occurring throughout the captivity in all of the stories. The humiliation and torture, both physical and psychological, and cruel treatment and killings of the Armenian POWS and civilians are violations against Geneva Conventions;[27] hence, the perpetrator, the government of the Republic of Azerbaijan, must pay the price of its brutal crimes.

Whether you are Armenian, of Armenian descent in the diaspora, or simply someone who cares deeply about shedding light on the brutal injustices still going on in our modern civilized world, the burden is on us to spread awareness in our communities. Each of us can play a small but important part by talking about these stories on social media or wherever we have the most influence. We can also reach out by email to human rights defenders, politicians, and journalists in our regions, pleading with them to make this urgent issue a global priority.

---

[26] Ad Hoc Public Report. Responsibility of Azerbaijan for Torture and Inhuman Treatment of Armenian Captives: Evidence-based Analysis (The 2020 Nagorno Karabakh War). September. 2021. Page 7. Online: https://www.ombuds.am/images/files/8f33e8ccaac978faac7f4cf10442f835.pdf

[27] Geneva Convention Relative To The Treatment Of Prisoners Of War Of 12 August 1949. Online: https://www.un.org/en/genocideprevention/documents/atrocity-crimes/Doc.32_GC-III-EN.pdf

It may not seem like there is much that any single person can do to change the outcome of large international political issues, but each of us can help make the public more aware of intolerable crimes against Armenians that have gone on for far too long. That awareness is what will lead to real change, hopefully sooner rather than later. Those Armenians still in Azerbaijani captivity are counting on us and cannot wait forever.

Members of the media may contact me about the contents of *Sadistic Pleasures* by email at silentcrimesofazerbaijan@gmail.com or on Facebook at https://www.facebook.com/silentcrimesofazerbaijan.

Ashkhen Arakelyan

CPSIA information can be obtained
at www.ICGtesting.com
Printed in the USA
BVHW042322230522
637882BV00006B/71/J